# Contents

# Listings

# Acknowledgements

The author would like to thank first of all his parents, who developed his taste for sciences in general and mathematics in particular, and who allowed him to dive into the world of computer science very early.

He does not forget either his wife or his two daughters, for having encouraged him in this solitary experiment that is the writing of a book. He hopes that his two daughters will soon be two readers interested in this book.

# Chapter 1

# Forewords

## 1.1 Constructionism

The best way to appropriate a subject is to play with it, to experiment, to make hypotheses, tests, in short to make sure that the comprehension, the internal model that our brain has built is indeed a representation, a faithful model of reality. This precept requires a laboratory, tools, which allow us to carry out these experiments, these tests and to validate these hypotheses.

It is a theory of learning that Papert Seymour conceived when he worked at the MIT Media Lab, to integrate new technologies into learning.

It is this precept, this approach, that will follow throughout this book to explain how Gradient Boosting methods work.

Machine Learning methods are all based on mathematical principles which are abstract by nature. Fortunately for the developer, the computer scientist, the toolbox, the natural laboratory for experimenting with these mathematical concepts is programming.

Programming gives substance to these theories, allows them to be applied to concrete cases, to test their limits and to display the results.

The juxtaposition of seemingly complex mathematical concepts with their implementation immediately demystifies the subject and greatly facilitates their understanding.

## 1.2 Objectives

Applied to the subject of this book, this approach will allow the reader to appropriate by practice, by experimentation, the method of Gradient Boosting applied to the construction of decision trees.

Each concept of this method will be illustrated in depth, not only with examples of application code, but above all with listings allowing them to be concretised.

The set of codes presented here allows us to rebuild from scratch a training library for Gradient Boosting methods, from training to prediction, including the automation of hyperparameters tuning and explicability. At the end of their reading and ideally of their execution and modification, the reader will have acquired a fine mastery of the subject.

## 1.3   Structure of the book

This book is structured according to a progressive plan, which starts from the basic principles of the Gradient Boosting method, tackled in the first chapter, and progressively addresses more and more advanced subjects.

The first chapter provides an introduction to the method, citing its applications, advantages and limitations.

The second chapter goes into the details of the mathematical theory, and proposes a minimal implementation to play with these concepts and ensure a complete understanding of their operation.

The third chapter details with code and graphics how to train a model, how to prepare data, which metrics to analyze, how to avoid overlearning.

The fourth chapter goes back to the importance of explicability, particularly with regard to the SHAP method. An implementation of this method but also of the classical approach is given.

The central topic of Hyper Parameter Tuning is the subject of the fifth chapter. The importance of this step is recalled, and in accordance with the constructionist approach of this book, an implementation of a Hyper Parameter Optimizer is presented.

The sixth chapter returns to a mathematical object at the heart of the Gradient Boosting approach: the objective function. The emphasis is put on the customisation of these functions which can bring additional accuracy to a model.

The question of the treatment of time series, which require adaptations to enter the framework of constant leaf decision trees, is treated in the seventh chapter.

The penultimate chapter compares the main existing libraries, namely the famous XGBoost, but also LightGBM and CatBoost. Each one has its own particularities which make them more adapted to a particular case. Finally, the last chapter briefly discusses the multi-model approach.

## 1.4 Getting the code

All the code examples of this book are available freely online. They are hosted in github, right here:

> ☞ github.com/kayhman/ PracticalGradientBoosting.

The author strongly advise the reader to play with them.

# Chapter 2

# Gradient Boosted Tree: context and theory

## 2.1 Context

This chapter outlines a first overview of Gradient Boosted Trees (GBT) models. These are predictive models, consisting of a set of decision trees, which are learned sequentially, boosting the accuracy of the previous model.

The prediction is generally of two types: regression or classification.

Classification analyses a set of data and assigns a label to it.

Regression analyses the data and produces a numerical value.

In this first section, we will provide some background information on data science and the place of Gradient Boosted Trees methods in it.

The situation in which they can be used will be the subject of the next section, while their advantages and limitations will be discussed in the next two sections.

### 2.1.1 Ocean of data

In every areas of human activity, the volume of data available has exploded over the last two decades: this is the Big Data revolution. This pool of data is a source of applications and progress that are just waiting to be exploited. The possible uses are legion.

On the other hand, this data is collected in such proportions that it is difficult, if not impossible, for a human being to grasp it.

In industry, it is now common to have to work with tens or even hundreds of billions of rows of data, with potentially hundreds or thousands of columns for each row.

The health sector is no exception, with the transposition of the volume between rows and columns. In this context, the data, attached anonymously to a patient, constitute few rows, because of the small number of patients. On the other hand, biological, physiological, clinical, and morphological metrics are numerous and end up generating a large number of columns.

No field escapes this digitization of data, and each one can benefit from the contributions of machine learning. Having tools such as Gradient Boosted Trees is a formidable accelerator.

### 2.1.2   What for?

The usefulness and value of this data are not necessarily immediately apparent. Classically, the possible uses of this data fall into two main categories:

- Regression applications, exploit large and ideally deep data histories to predict an event or a value. The application domains are multiple and range from the prediction of traffic on a network to the anticipation of the occurrence of an epileptic seizure, throught the simulation of the behavior of a wind turbine.

- Classification applications, take advantage of the representativeness offered by large data sets to learn to recognize various patterns in data. Here again, the spectrum of uses is vast and covers fields as varied as the identification of tumors in scanner images, the recognition of flowers, or the detection of pathological electrocardiograms.

Many other forms of use outside of these two broad categories are possible, even though it is almost always possible to reduce them to these two categories.

One example is generative methods, generally based on neural networks, which can produce paintings in the style of a specific artist. The latter can be seen as a form of prediction, which based on input characteristics, predicts the painting that the artist would have made.

The figure above is a very good illustration of an application that goes beyond the prediction/categorization framework and highlights the change in dimension brought about by Big Data.

It shows the generation of a map of the New York transport network based solely on the coordinates for getting into and out of a taxi.

The creation of this map is only made possible by the huge volume of data.

### 2.1.3  Efficiency issues

To cope with this volume of this data, since the mid-1990s, thanks to the generalization of computer tools and the acceleration of computer processing speed, increasingly sophisticated methods have appeared.

Two main lines of research have been fruitfully explored to meet this need for modelization:

- Methods based on simple models with many parameters. The abundance of parameters to be identified during learning requires the use of powerful machines, usually GPUs. Deep neural networks are an example of such methods. Note that in data scientist jargon, these methods are more commonly referred to as regressive methods. The order of magnitude for the number of parameters to be determined is in the tens to hundreds of millions.

- Methods based on more complicated models, with fewer parameters to be identified during the learning phases. The lower number of parameters to be learned during the training of the models makes them less demanding in terms of computing power, but the underlying mathematics can be more complex.

Of course, the boundary between these two types of methods is thin, and it is increasingly common to see complex methods requiring the learning of many parameters and therefore involving long learning times.

The Gradient Boosting methods explored in this book fall into the second category. Their interest and success are partly due to the great efficiency they derive from the complexity of their model, which allows them to capture the complexity of reality. The small number of parameters contributes to accelerating the learning time.

## 2.2   Case of application of the Gradient Boosting methods

### 2.2.1   Recognised track record

Gradient Boosting methods have proven to be particularly effective tools in the world of Data Science. The various libraries that implement their principles, such as XGBoost, CatBoost, or Light-GBM, are regularly at the top of the list of best solutions in Data Science competitions such as Kaggle.

Their generality, speed of training, and versatility have led to their widespread use in many fields, including industrial, commercial, energetical, and medical.

### 2.2.2   Broad spectrum of applications

Gradient Boosting methods have the added advantage of being used with equal success in the two major use cases of machine learning mentioned above: regression and classification.

This is one of their great strengths and the reason for their versatility. Mastering Gradient Boosting methods, therefore, allows one to successfully tackle multiple data science problems. It would be a shame to miss out on this gain in efficiency in the field of data science, where there are already many difficulties.

This bivalence has its limitations, of course, but in the following chapters, we will present the means available to remedy them.

### 2.2.3 Focus on structured data

Being essentially based on a decision tree approach, and thus on comparisons between values of a particular dimension of the training dataset, Gradient Boosting methods are applied to structured data.

When we talk about structured data, we are referring to data in tabular form, i.e. represented by tables. Each row of the table characterizes a record, a measurement, or an observation, and has several columns to describe it.

This form of data is commonplace and can be found in all fields. It is in this form that a large part of the data concerning all human activities is stored. In concrete terms, it is this type of data that is found in our databases, or CSV or Excel-type files.

Opposed to this is unstructured data, such as images, video, sound recordings, sensor measurements, 3D point clouds, etc. In other words, any form of data that does not take the form of a table with columns with precise content.

However, Gradient Boosting methods are not powerless against this type of data. The common trick to circumvent this limitation is to extract features from this unstructured data.

On images, it is possible to create a table where each image is a row, and each column is the result of the application of a particular filter. The same principle applies to any 1D signal. A column can then be the energy for a specific frequency band, the coefficient of a Fourier series, or a wavelet transform.

The scientific literature is full of examples where this method has been applied with convincing results.

It is therefore also possible to use Gradient Boosted Trees in this context.

## 2.3 Undeniable advantages

The previous sections have highlighted some of the advantages of Gradient Boosting methods. This section goes into more detail on each of them.

### 2.3.1 Simplicity of configuration

The first undeniable advantage of these methods lies in their simplicity of use. Whatever the library or language used, generally Python, creating a first model does not require more than a few lines of code.

The parameters accessible to the user are, for the most part, easy to understand, and easily optimized in the hyperparameter tuning phase. The Hyper Parameter Tuning chapter will go into this point in greater detail.

### 2.3.2 Polyvalence

Gradient Boosting methods shine by their versatility. As written above, they natively support classification as well as regression.

Moreover, they excel in both domains and have demonstrated their ability to achieve significant levels of accuracy in both cases.

As proof, they regularly find themselves at the top of the rankings in Kaggle-type data science contests.

### 2.3.3 Interpretability

One point that is regularly overlooked when choosing a model type is its interpretability. This is an essential factor to take into account, not only by the data scientist to refine his understanding of a problem but also by the final recipient of the model.

The latter will need to trust the prediction or classification output of the model. Having a rationale for the output is crucial.

Due to their structure, based on decision trees, it is possible to interpret the output of Gradient Boosting methods. Depending on the implementation chosen, various indicators or graphs are provided to facilitate this appropriation of the model.

Finally, their very specific structure allows optimizations that enable the application of NP-complete explainability methods such as SHAP while keeping a polynomial computation time. The chapter on interpretability will return to this point.

### 2.3.4 Large capacity of ingestion

As mentioned at the beginning of this chapter: the mass of data available to the data scientist is constantly growing. Having a model that is mathematically powerful but does not scale is rarely interesting. Support Vector Machine (SVM) type methods suffer from this pitfall. They are particularly efficient, but beyond 10,000 rows of data, their training time becomes prohibitive.

Fortunately, this is not the case for Gradient Boosting methods, which are distinguished by very good performance during training. This good performance is due to the low algorithmic complexity and the possibility of parallelizing part of the calculations.

This possibility of parallelization is particularly attractive because it allows the distribution of the training across a cluster of computers, which authorizes the use of really important volumes of data.

### 2.3.5 Great robustness

The inherent malleability of using decision trees as the underlying model is a guarantee of robustness for Gradient Boosting methods.

As will be seen in the next chapter, where their principles and operation are discussed, the combination of multiple decision trees, specially adapted to the data during training, allows their structure to be finely tuned and to emerge.

This gives them a low sensitivity to the data, and guarantees that a model parameterized for one use case will not see its accuracy collapse once it is trained on another set of data. This is true as long as over-fitting is avoided.

### 2.3.6 Customisation

Although they provide satisfactory performance by default on many use cases, it is nonetheless possible to push this type of model to its limits to obtain additional precision, sometimes vital for a use case.

To this end, partly thanks to the mathematical formalization of this type of method, it is possible to surgically refine several steps. In the chapter Defining custom objectives, the issue of specializing a model for a particular business need will be addressed.

### 2.3.7 Very good level of precision

Finally, and most importantly, Gradient Boosting methods deliver very high levels of accuracy on the classifications or regressions they perform.

This is ultimately their main strength, responsible for their wide diffusion.

## 2.4 Limitations

Despite all these advantages, Gradient Boosting methods applied to decision tree training do suffer from some limitations.

### 2.4.1 Lack of support for extrapolation

As will be demonstrated in the next chapter, Gradient Boosting methods based on decision trees cannot intrinsically extrapolate.

This can be a concern when it is necessary to create a model capable of making predictions in a temporal context where the data are not stationary.

That is, they are subject to non-periodic variations over time, such as continuous growth or decay. Some of these are fortunately circumventable. The following chapters will propose some palliatives.

## 2.4.2   No features engineering

Neural networks, despite the reservations which are expressed about their configuration and training time and their insatiable appetite for data, nevertheless present a characteristic that makes them unique: they are capable of constructing high-level features from raw features.

In Gradient Boosting methods, nothing similar exists. The initial data are kept as they are, and no enrichment is done.

On the other hand, they are capable of separating the chaff from the wheat, and therefore can discard features that are not relevant.

This automatic sorting of features according to their relevance allows these models to be fed with a maximum number of features, with the algorithm taking care to retain the relevant ones.

# Chapter 3

# Gradient Boosted Trees: Under the hood

## 3.1 Ensemble methods

After the high-level overview offered by the first chapter on Gradient Boosting methods applied to decision trees, this section will provide an opportunity to get to the heart of the subject, by detailing the principles and methods on which they are based.

After a reminder of the motivations justifying the use of ensemble models and their construction with a Gradient Boosting approach, this chapter will discuss the functioning of decision trees. These are the basic models underlying Gradient Boosted Tree methods.

The section on Gradient Boosting will present the mathematical foundations of this approach and will propose an implementation in python for decision trees. Coding their operation, both for training and prediction will give substance to these theoretical explanations.

### 3.1.1 Principles and motivations

Gradient Boosted Tree models are to be classified in the category of ensemble methods. The base of these methods is to build complex models by combining sets of simpler models. The model thus obtained is called a strong learner, while the sub-models composing it are called weak learners.

These methods have proved to be particularly successful and have been the subject of numerous scientific publications, both on the type of underlying model used and on the algorithms for training and intelligently combining these underlying models.

In the case of Gradient Boosted Trees, decision trees are used as weak predictors, while the Gradient Boosting method is applied for training.

The sections Decision Trees and Gradient Boosting will discuss these two elements in depth.

## Minimal example

We will look at a first example to illustrate the ensemble approach.

One of the simplest models that can be realized with an ensemblistic method is the linear spline model. In this example, the weak predictors are simple regression lines.

Using only one of them gives very poor results for a somewhat complex problem. However, by combining several of these lines, it is possible to obtain very good results.

The following listing illustrates this by showing how it is possible to combine a set of lines to create a predictor for the logarithm function:

Listing 3.1: spline.py

```python
# spline.py
import numpy as np
import math
import random
from numpy.linalg import inv

import matplotlib.pyplot as plt

nbSamples = 30

X = np.matrix([[(x + 1) * 1.0 / nbSamples, 1]
               for x in range(nbSamples)])
Y = np.matrix([math.log(x[0].item(0))
               for x in X]).transpose()


def Iplus(xi, x):
    if x >= xi:
        return x - xi
    else:
        return 0.0


def splinify(xMin, xMax, step, x):
    a = [
        Iplus(xMin + i * step, x)
        for i in range(int((xMax - xMin) / step))
    ]
    a.reverse()
```

```python
    return a + [1]


Xsplines = np.matrix([
    splinify(0.0, 1.0, 1, x[0].item(0)) for x in X
])
A = inv(Xsplines.transpose() *
        Xsplines) * Xsplines.transpose() * Y
YregLine = np.matrix([[np.dot(x, A).item(0)]
                    for x in Xsplines])


Xsplines = np.matrix([
    splinify(0.0, 1.0, 0.5, x[0].item(0))
    for x in X
])
A = inv(Xsplines.transpose() *
        Xsplines) * Xsplines.transpose() * Y
YregCoarse = np.matrix([[np.dot(x, A).item(0)]
                    for x in Xsplines])


Xsplines = np.matrix([
    splinify(0.0, 1.0, 0.05, x[0].item(0))
    for x in X
])
A = inv(Xsplines.transpose() *
        Xsplines) * Xsplines.transpose() * Y
Yreg = np.matrix([[np.dot(x, A).item(0)]
                    for x in Xsplines])


plt.style.use('grayscale')
plt.plot(np.asarray(X[:, 0]),
        np.asarray(Y),
        '+',
        label='Value to predict(log)')
plt.plot(np.asarray(X[:, 0]),
        np.asarray(YregLine),
        label='Linear regression')
plt.plot(np.asarray(X[:, 0]),
        np.asarray(YregCoarse),
        label='2 splines')
plt.plot(np.asarray(X[:, 0]),
        np.asarray(Yreg),
        label='20 splines')
plt.legend(loc="upper left")
plt.savefig('spline.png')
plt.show()
```

The first few lines of code simply load the modules that are useful for our demonstration, namely NumPy for matrix calculations and algebra. Matplotlib is used to display the curves.

The last few lines show the log curve compared to the strong predictors, with more and more splines. The curves become closer as the number of splines increases, as shown in the figure below:

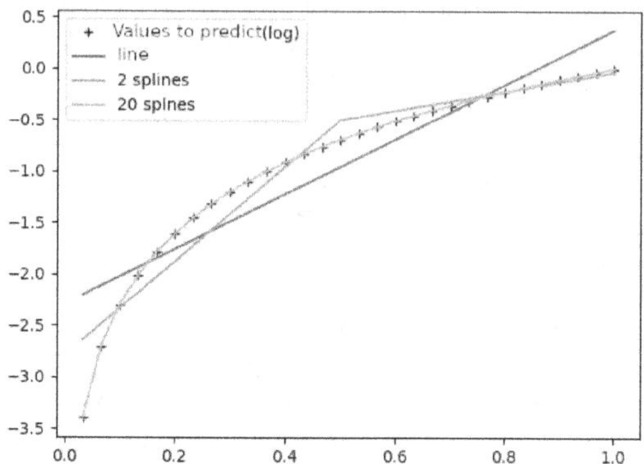


This example shows that the ensemblist approach is effective, even for modeling non-linear phenomena with linear sub-models.

## 3.2   Decision trees

Decision trees are the weak predictors used by the Gradient Boosted Trees models presented in this book. It is by combining them that they constitute a strong predictor. The following paragraphs detail their operation and give a first simple implementation in Python.

### 3.2.1   Principles and motivations

Decision trees are a simple but very powerful data structure that allows, as the name suggests, to access a value based on a series of decisions.

Each node of the tree is associated with a decision. These decisions, calling only for a positive or negative response, are binary. Each node, therefore, has two child nodes. These are therefore binary trees. These nodes can be a leaf or another decision node.

The following diagram illustrates this principle for a tree that compares data consisting of two columns: A and B. Depending on the value of these two columns, the predicted values will be 2, 4, or 6.

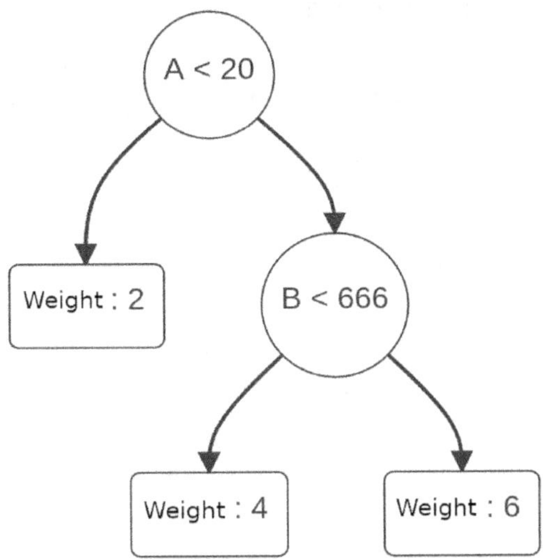



By convention, and throughout the rest of this book, binary trees will be interpreted as follows:

- Nodes are represented by circles

- Leaves are rectangles

- Nodes contain a binary test. If the test is positive, the tree continues on the left branch. If it is negative, the tree continues on the right branch

- The leaves contain the weights, i.e. the predicted values

- It is important to note that the depth of a decision tree, through the number of leaves, will govern the cardinality of the prediction space. This is in contrast to prediction methods derived from linear regression methods, which generate continuous predictions.

The table below clarifies the functioning of this structure within the framework of the tree presented in the previous figure:

| A | B | Decision (weight) |
|---|---|---|
| 18 | 5 | 2 |
| 18 | 155 | 2 |
| 23 | 555 | 4 |
| 23 | 777 | 6 |

## 3.2.2   Minimal example

The following listing shows how to code a decision tree in a few
lines.  It starts by defining a DecisionNode class representing a
node:

Listing 3.2: decision_node.py

```python
# decision node.py
class DecisionNode:
    """

    Node decision class.
    This is a simple binary node,
    with potentially two children:
      left and right
    Left node is returned when condition is true
    False node is returned when condition is false
    """

    def __init__(self,
                 name,
                 condition,
                 value=None):
        self.name = name
        self.condition = condition
        self.value = value
        self.left = None
        self.right = None

    def add_left_node(self, left):
        self.left = left

    def add_right_node(self, right):
        self.right = right

    def is_leaf(self):
        """
        Node is a leaf if it has no child
        """
        return (not self.left) and (
            not self.right)

    def next(self, data):
        """
        Return next node depending on
        data and node condition
        """
        cond = self.condition(data)
        if cond:
            return self.left
        else:
            return self.right
```

This class implements two methods to add a right and a left node: add_right_node and add_left_node respectively. is_leaf informs the developer that it is a leaf node, while next allows the navigation to the next node according to the input data and the condition.

The condition is added at creation time, in the form of a function that takes the data as input and returns true or false. An example is given below.

A second class, DecisionTree is then defined:

Listing 3.3: decision_tree.py

```python
# decision_tree.py
class DecisionTree:
    """
    A DecisionTree is a model that
    provides predictions depending on input.
    A Prediction is the sum of the leaves' values,
    for those leaves that were activated
    by the input
    """

    def __init__(self, root):
        """
        A DecisionTree is defined by an objective,
        a number of estimators and a max depth.
        """
        self.root = root

    def predict(self, data):
        child = self.root
        while child and not child.is_leaf():
            child = child.next(data)
        return child.value
```

It is constructed by taking a root node and is responsible for predicting by traversing the tree from that root, taking into account the data.

The following code implements the tree shown in Figure 1. and ensures that the predicted values are the expected ones:

Listing 3.4: decision_tree_example.py

```python
# decision_tree_example.py
from decision_node import DecisionNode
from decision_tree import DecisionTree

root = DecisionNode('root',
                lambda d: d['A'] < 20.0)
root_left = DecisionNode('root_left', None, 2)
root_right = DecisionNode(
```

```python
    'root_right', lambda d: d['B'] < 666.0, None)
left_left = DecisionNode('left_left', None, 4)
left_right = DecisionNode('left_right', None, 6)

root.add_left_node(root_left)
root.add_right_node(root_right)

root_right.add_left_node(left_left)
root_right.add_right_node(left_right)

tree = DecisionTree(root)
print(tree.predict({'A': 18, 'B': 5}))    # 2
print(tree.predict({'A': 18, 'B': 155}))  # 2
print(tree.predict({'A': 23, 'B': 555}))  # 4
print(tree.predict({'A': 23, 'B': 777}))  # 6
```

The 5 nodes of our example tree are first created, before being added using add_left_node and add_right_node.

Three of these nodes are leaves and do not contain a decision function. The other two are nodes themselves and have no values, but decision functions.

The tree is then constructed by specifying the root node. Finally, the predictions are obtained by calling the predict method of the DecisionTree class. The predicted values are indeed the expected ones.

### 3.2.3   Ensemble of decision trees

Decision trees are a powerful tool, capable of capturing the structure of complex data sets.

However, this compliance with the data comes sometimes at the expense of simplicity, by imposing the use of very deep trees with many nodes.

One way of limiting this effect, while gaining in precision, is to use an ensemblist approach, as has been shown for splines.

The decision tree below associates each number between 1 and 4 inclusive with its own value. A 1 in input gives a 1, a 2 a two, ...

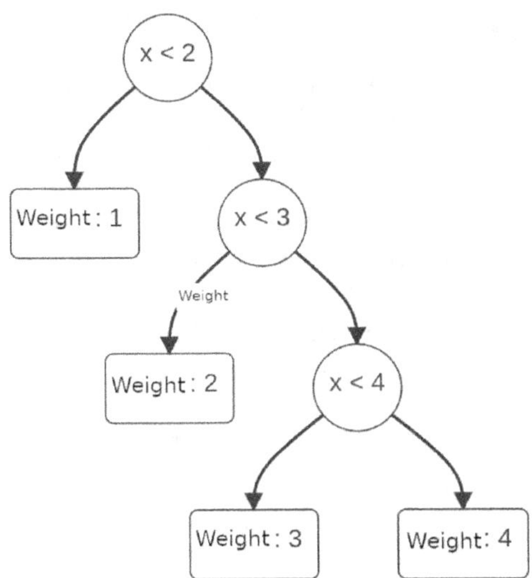



Using the DecisionNode and DecisionTree classes presented above, it can be implemented as follows:

Listing 3.5: tree_ensemble.py

```python
# tree_ensemble.py
from decision_node import DecisionNode
from decision_tree import DecisionTree

L0 = DecisionNode('L0', lambda d: d['x'] < 2)
L1_L = DecisionNode('L1_L', None, 1)
L1_R = DecisionNode('L1_R', lambda d: d['x'] < 3,
                    None)
L2_L = DecisionNode('L2_L', None, 2)
L2_R = DecisionNode('L2_R', lambda d: d['x'] < 4,
                    None)
L3_L = DecisionNode('L3_L', None, 3)
L3_R = DecisionNode('L3_R', None, 4)

L0.add_left_node(L1_L)
L0.add_right_node(L1_R)

L1_R.add_left_node(L2_L)
L1_R.add_right_node(L2_R)

L2_R.add_left_node(L3_L)
L2_R.add_right_node(L3_R)

tree = DecisionTree(L0)
print(tree.predict({'x': 1}))  # 1
print(tree.predict({'x': 2}))  # 2
print(tree.predict({'x': 3}))  # 3
```

```
print(tree.predict({'x': 4}))  # 4
```

This is a model of our prediction problem built with a single tree, forming a strong predictor on its own.

The same problem can be tackled with a ensemble approach, by limiting the depth of the trees in our set to two levels. Such a tree has only two leaves, and therefore cannot predict more than two values. It is therefore necessary to combine several such trees to obtain a strong predictor.

The figure below shows how this can be done using 3 weak predictors:

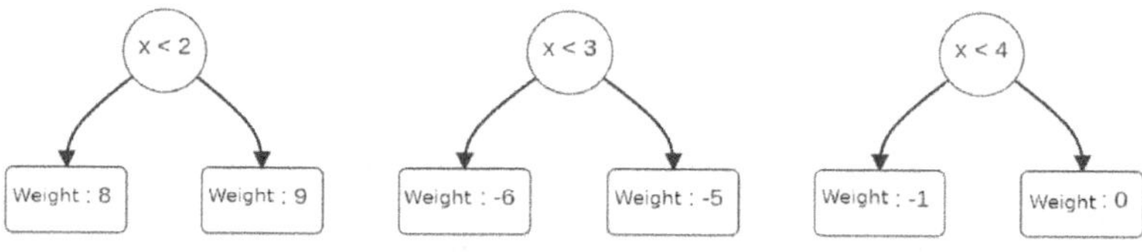


Each of these predictors taken individually gives very poor results. Independently, none of them makes an accurate prediction, for any of the numbers between 1 and 4 inclusive.

However, if they are simply combined, by summing them, then they give the exact result. The listing below demonstrates this:

Listing 3.6: tree_ensemble_weak.py

```
# tree_ensemble_weak.py
from decision_node import DecisionNode
from decision_tree import DecisionTree

T0_L0 = DecisionNode('L0', lambda d: d['x'] < 2)
T0_L1_L = DecisionNode('L1_L', None, 8)
T0_L1_R = DecisionNode('L1_R', None, 9)

T1_L0 = DecisionNode('L0', lambda d: d['x'] < 3)
T1_L1_L = DecisionNode('L1_L', None, -6)
```

```python
T1_L1_R = DecisionNode('L1_R', None, -5)

T2_L0 = DecisionNode('L0', lambda d: d['x'] < 4)
T2_L1_L = DecisionNode('L1_L', None, -1)
T2_L1_R = DecisionNode('L1_R', None, 0)

T0_L0.add_left_node(T0_L1_L)
T0_L0.add_right_node(T0_L1_R)

T1_L0.add_left_node(T1_L1_L)
T1_L0.add_right_node(T1_L1_R)

T2_L0.add_left_node(T2_L1_L)
T2_L0.add_right_node(T2_L1_R)

T0 = DecisionTree(T0_L0)
T1 = DecisionTree(T1_L0)
T2 = DecisionTree(T2_L0)

strong_predictor = lambda x: T0.predict(
    x) + T1.predict(x) + T2.predict(x)

print(strong_predictor({'x': 1}))  # 1
print(strong_predictor({'x': 2}))  # 2
print(strong_predictor({'x': 3}))  # 3
print(strong_predictor({'x': 4}))  # 4
```

This code begins by creating each of the weak predictors, as defined in the figure above. The strong predictor is constructed by simply joining these three trees using a sum. The resulting prediction is then precisely the expected one.

## 3.3   Gradient boosting

The structure, manual creation, and running of a decision tree have been described above, this new section will detail how to build and combine these weak predictors to build a strong predictor.

This construction and assembly is the complex part when building a model according to the Gradient Boosted Tree method: one has to identify the decision criteria for each node, calculate the optimal value for each leaf, and then start again for the next predictor.

This is the learning phase of the model. It should ingest the data from the training set and extract the optimal parameters.

In the following paragraphs, we will go into the mathematical principles and methods that are used to ensure this construction.

### 3.3.1 Principle of boosting

Gradient boosting methods derive, as their name suggests, from the boosting method. The principle of boosting consists of two points:

- Sequentially combining weak models to build a strong model

- Train each of these models on a modified version of the training data

The originality of this approach lies essentially in the second point, the idea being to focus on the new predictor where the previous ones lacked precision.

This is generally done by giving more weight during training to data samples for which the error is large. Other treatments can be applied to alter the data between successive trainings. Using the gradient of an error function is one of them and the one on which Gradient Boosting is based.

In the final step, the set of weak predictors thus obtained is combined by weighting each model proportionally to its accuracy.

### 3.3.2 Mathematical foundations

Mathematics is a necessary tool for carrying out a task as complex as the constitution of a set of decision trees and guarantee a reliable prediction.

Firstly, they allow the problem to be posed in a formal, rigorous, and exploitable manner. Secondly, once the problem has been posed, it is possible to use the mathematical toolbox to provide an optimal solution.

The following sections specify the parameters to be identified to construct the trees, then quantify the impact of these parameters on the prediction by introducing the notion of objective, and finally explain how to find the optimal parameters for a given objective.

### Parameters

The figure below shows the shape of a simple decision tree:

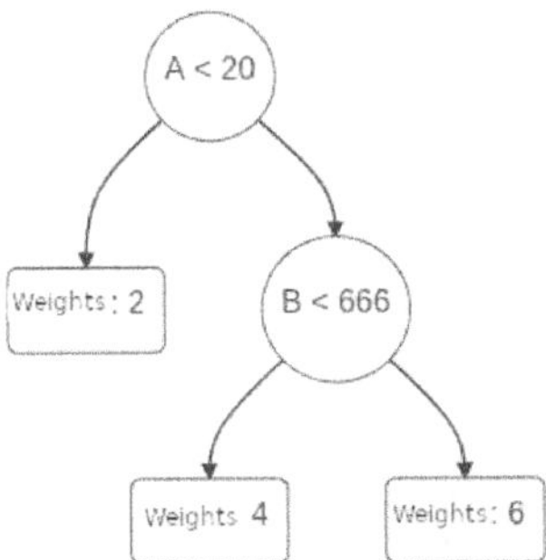


It appears from this diagram that there are at least three parameters to be defined during the learning process:

- The variables considered for the decisions at each node, here A or B

- The decision criteria attached to each node. Here be less than 20 or 666.

- The weights of each leaf, which will be the basis of each prediction. Here 2, 4, or 6.

Gradient Boosting provides a mathematically sound approach to choosing the best values for each of these parameters.

## Objective function

The first tool to be defined is the objective function. This is a mathematical function that will allow the quality of a predictor to be quantified and objectified with respect to the training data.

Essentially, it measures the error between the values predicted by the model and the real values. Several choices are possible, depending on whether it is a classification or a regression, on the business objective that is being pursued, and on the mathematical properties that are useful for the method employed.

In the case of Gradient Boosting methods, the objective function must be derivable, otherwise, it is impossible to calculate a gradient.

The chapter on the proper use of objective functions will provide an opportunity to go into more detail on the various options available to the data scientist. However, the Mean Squared Error (MSE) is standard for regression problems, and the logistic error for binary classifications.

The listing below concretizes this concept of the objective function for the case of the regression performed in the previous section, which employed a ensemble approach:

Listing 3.7: regression_objective.py

```python
# regression_objective.py
import numpy as np

from decision_node import DecisionNode
from decision_tree import DecisionTree

T0_L0 = DecisionNode('L0', lambda d: d['x'] < 2)
T0_L1_L = DecisionNode('L1_L', None, 8)
T0_L1_R = DecisionNode('L1_R', None, 9)

T1_L0 = DecisionNode('L0', lambda d: d['x'] < 3)
T1_L1_L = DecisionNode('L1_L', None, -6)
T1_L1_R = DecisionNode('L1_R', None, -5)

T2_L0 = DecisionNode('L0', lambda d: d['x'] < 4)
T2_L1_L = DecisionNode('L1_L', None, -1)
T2_L1_R = DecisionNode('L1_R', None, 0)

T0_L0.add_left_node(T0_L1_L)
T0_L0.add_right_node(T0_L1_R)

T1_L0.add_left_node(T1_L1_L)
T1_L0.add_right_node(T1_L1_R)

T2_L0.add_left_node(T2_L1_L)
T2_L0.add_right_node(T2_L1_R)

T0 = DecisionTree(T0_L0)
T1 = DecisionTree(T1_L0)
T2 = DecisionTree(T2_L0)

strong_predictor = lambda x: T0.predict(
    x) + T1.predict(x) + T2.predict(x)

squared_error = lambda y_true, y_pred: (y_true -
                                        y_pred)**2
x_train = [1, 2, 3, 4]
y_train = [1, 2, 3, 4]

T0_mse = np.mean([
    squared_error(x, T0.predict({'x': x}))
    for x, y in zip(x_train, y_train)
])
T1_mse = np.mean([
    squared_error(x, T1.predict({'x': x}))
    for x, y in zip(x_train, y_train)
])
T2_mse = np.mean([
    squared_error(x, T2.predict({'x': x}))
    for x, y in zip(x_train, y_train)
```

```python
])

strong_mse = np.mean([
    squared_error(x, strong_predictor({'x': x}))
    for x, y in zip(x_train, y_train)
])

print(T0_mse)       # 39.75
print(T1_mse)       # 64.5
print(T2_mse)       # 11.25
print(strong_mse)   # 0.0
```

This code uses the MSE, i.e. the mean square error, to calculate the error for the test data. It is implemented here in two steps, first defining the squared_error function which calculates the square of the error, and then averaging it for all the test points with the mean function of NumPy.

This function is then applied to each of the weak predictors and the strong predictor coupling the weak predictors.

This verifies that the three weak predictors, taken individually, generate a large error, while the strong predictor has a zero error.

In essence, the objective function allows the quality of a model to be quantified against a data set. The following section will show how to use an objective function to identify the optimal parameters of a decision tree.

## Optimisation

Objective functions are therefore precise, rigorous, and flexible mathematical means of quantifying the quality of a predictor. However, this is not their only interest.

If they are continuous and twice derivable with respect to the parameters we are trying to determine, then it becomes possible to use them to optimize and identify the parameters that minimize or maximize this function.

Now, among the three parameters mentioned above, and to be identified during the training of a decision tree, the last one, namely the weight of each leaf, is found directly in the objective function. It is the predicted value and therefore the value that is subtracted from the true value.

Mathematically, and in a generic way, the objective functions are defined according to this formula:

$$obj^{(t)} = \sum_{i=1}^{n} l(y_i, \hat{y}_i^{(t)}) + \sum_{i=1}^{t} \Omega(f_i)$$

With l being the loss function. It is ultimately a function that calculates a type of error, such as the square of the error in our previous example.

The Omega term, on the other hand, is a model regularisation function whose purpose is to control the complexity of the model. The Hyper Parameters chapter will discuss this in more detail. Briefly, Omega limits overfitting by penalizing models that are too specific and generalize poorly.

It often takes the following form:

$$\Omega(f) = \gamma T + \frac{1}{2}\lambda \sum_{j=1}^{T} w_j^2$$

With T being the number of leaves in the tree and $w_j$ being the weights of the leaves. Gamma and Lambda weigh their importance. Forcing the minimization of Omega then amounts to favoring trees with few leaves and low weights, with Gamma and Lambda being positive.

The objective itself is calculated by summing the loss function for each row of the training data, while Omega is applied to each tree in the set and then added to the whole.

For computational simplicity, the objective function is then linearised using its Taylor series expansion to order 2:

$$obj^{(t)} = \sum_{i=1}^{n} l(y_i, \hat{y}_i^{(t-1)}) + g_i f_t(x_i) + \frac{1}{2}h_i f_t^2(x_i) + \Omega(f_t) + constant$$

where the terms $g_i$ and $h_i$ are respectively the first derivative, i.e. the gradient, and the second derivative, i.e. the hessian:

$$g_i = \partial_{\hat{y}^{(t-1)}} l(y_i, \hat{y}_i^{(t-1)})$$

$$h_i = \partial_{\hat{y}^{(t-1)}}^2 l(y_i, \hat{y}_i^{(t-1)})$$

Removing the constant terms, which will not be involved in minimizing the objective, the following formula emerges:

$$\sum_{i=1}^{n} \left[ g_i f_t(x_i) + \frac{1}{2}h_i f_t^2(x_i) \right] + \Omega(f_t)$$

It is this sum that must be minimized with respect to the weight of the leaves of our trees. After deriving it with respect to these weights, and looking for the weight values canceling this derivative, the following weight value emerges:

$$w_j^* = -\frac{G_j}{H_j + \lambda}$$

Where $G_j$ is the sum of the gradients applied to the data attached to node $j$, and $H_j$ is the sum of the Hessian applied to the data attached to node j.

In the end, the formula giving the optimal value for the weight of a branch is not only simple but also very generic. Any loss function can be used, provided that it is twice derivable, i.e. that it is possible to calculate the gradient and the Hessian.

### Interpretation

Before going into the details of a Python implementation, it is necessary to return to this last formula to understand its meaning and to understand what the weights of the leaves of the decision trees contain.

In particular, the case where the loss function l is the squared error is instructive. As a reminder, the squared error is formulated as follows:

$$l(y_i, \hat{y}_i) = (y_i - \hat{y}_i)^2$$

Its derivative with respect to the prediction $\hat{y}$, the Gradient, is straightforward, and gives :

$$-2(y_i - \hat{y}_i)$$

The second derivative, the Hessian, which is also the derivative of the Gradient, then becomes the constant :

$$2$$

By carrying over these two terms into the calculation of the optimal weight w* for a leaf, and by taking 0 for the lambda regularisation term, it appears that the weights w* are none other than double the sum of the errors of each line of the training dataset divided by 2 * the number of lines.

It is therefore simply the opposite of the average of the errors attached to a leaf, compared to the previous prediction, which is assigned to the weight of a leaf. The previous prediction is therefore corrected by the average of the errors.

### 3.3.3  Minimal implementation

After a detailed overview of the formulas used to assign the most relevant weights to the leaves of a decision tree, this section will now focus on explaining how to translate these abstract mathematics into Python code.

This will allow us to understand exactly what happens when training a set of decision trees to be able to parameterize them intelligently.

## DecisionSet class

The listings below code the training of a set of decision trees:

Listing 3.8: train_ensemble_tree.py

```python
import matplotlib.pyplot as plt
import pandas as pd
from jax import grad, jacfwd, jacrev, jit
import jax.numpy as jnp
import numpy as np

import random


class DecisionNode:
    """
    Node decision class.
    This is a simple binary node, with potentially
    two childs: left and right
    Left node is returned when condition is true
    False node is returned when condition is false
    """

    def __init__(self,
                name,
                condition,
                value=None,
                depth=0,
                label=None):
        self.name = name
        self.condition = condition
        self.label = label
        self.value = value
        self.left = None
        self.right = None
        self.depth = depth

    def add_left_node(self,
                    left):
        self.left = left

    def add_right_node(self,
                    right):
        self.right = right

    def is_leaf(self):
```

```
        """
        Node is a leaf if it has no child
        """
    return (
        not self.left) and (
            not self.right)

def next(self, data):
    """
    Return next code depending on data
    and node condition
    """
    cond = self.condition(
        data)
    if cond:
      return self.left
    else:
      return self.right
```

The preceding lines take up the data structure which had been created upstream to define a node of the decision tree.

Note the import of the JAX library, which is an automatic differentiation library that will allow automation of the calculation of the gradient and the Hessian. Thanks to this, the code for the computation of the Hessian lies in two lines:

Listing 3.9: train_ensemble_tree.py

```
def hessian(fun):
  return jit(
     jacfwd(jacrev(fun)))
```

by applying the calculation of the Jacobian twice. These automatic differentiation primitives will allow the Gradient and Hessian to be calculated automatically, accurately, and generically, whatever the objective function.

This is extremely valuable when experimenting with different objective functions. With this tool, it becomes possible to extend the DecisionEnsemble class presented above to include the two calculators grad and hessian:

Listing 3.10: train_ensemble_tree.py

```
class DecisionEnsemble:
    """
    A DecisionEnsemble is a model
    that provides predictions depending on input.
    Prediction is the sum of the values attached
    to leaf activated by input
    """

    def __init__(self,
```

```python
            objective,
            nb_estimators,
            max_depth,
            gamma=0,
            lbda=0):
    """
    A DecisionEnsemble is defined by
    an objective,
    a number of estimators
    and a max depth.
    """
    self.roots = [
        DecisionNode(
            f'root_{esti}',
            None, 0.0)
        for esti in range(
            0, nb_estimators)
    ]
    self.objective = objective
    self.lbda = lbda
    self.gamma = gamma
    self.grad = grad(
        self.objective)
    self.hessian = hessian(
        self.objective)
    self.max_depth = max_depth
    self.base_score = None
```

The constructor of the class initializes some variables useful for training, notably the objective function and its derivatives, but also the list of root nodes, roots. Each of these nodes will be the root of the estimators in the ensemble. The prediction code remains unchanged:

Listing 3.11: train_ensemble_tree.py

```python
def predict(self, data):
  preds = []
  for _, row in data.iterrows(
  ):
    pred = 0.0
    for tree_idx, root in enumerate(
        self.roots):
      child = root
      while child and not child.is_leaf(
      ):
        child = child.next(
            row)
      # don't count base_score twice
      # for root node
      if child != root:
        pred += child.value
```

```python
        preds.append(pred)
    return np.array(
        preds
    ) + self.base_score
```

Initially, the presented code manually added the conditions in each of the tree nodes. As this step has now been delegated to the training, the _create_condition method has been added to the class:

Listing 3.12: train_ensemble_tree.py

```python
def _create_condition(
    self, col_name,
    split_value):
    """
    Create a closure that capture split value
    """
    return lambda dta: dta[
        col_name
    ] < split_value
```

Indeed, since the decision tree is binary, at least two values are needed for the filtering by the condition to be relevant. Finally, the _add_child_nodes method is introduced to add a new node as well as its children:

Listing 3.13: train_ensemble_tree.py

```python
def _add_child_nodes(
    self, node, nodes,
    node_x, node_y,
    split_value,
    split_column, nb_nodes,
    left_w, right_w,
    prev_w):
    node.condition = self._create_condition(
        split_column,
        split_value
    ) # we must create a closure to capture
      # split_value copy
    node.label = f'{split_column} < {split_value}'
    node.add_left_node(
        DecisionNode(
            f'left_{nb_nodes}',
            None,
            left_w + prev_w,
            depth=node.depth +
            1))
    node.add_right_node(
        DecisionNode(
            f'right_{nb_nodes}',
            None,
            right_w + prev_w,
```

```
                    depth=node.depth +
                    1))
        mask = node_x[
            split_column] < split_value
        # Reverse order to ensure bfs
        nodes.append(
            (node.left,
             node_x[mask].copy(),
             node_y[mask].copy(),
             left_w + prev_w))
        nodes.append(
            (node.right,
             node_x[~mask].copy(),
             node_y[~mask].copy(),
             right_w + prev_w))
```

The condition is created using the _create_condition function shown above. This creates a closure to capture the variable passed as a parameter. The right and left nodes are then added.

The following method, fit, forms the heart of this class and provides the training.

It takes two datasets as parameters: the one containing the training characteristics, x_train, and the one containing the values to be predicted, y_train.

Listing 3.14: train_ensemble_tree.py

```
def fit(self, x_train,
        y_train):
    """
    Fit decision trees using x_train and objective
    """
    self.base_score = y_train.mean(
    )
    self.roots[
        0].value = self.base_score
    node_count = 0
    for tree_idx, tree_root in enumerate(
        self.roots):
        # store current node (currenly a lead), x_train
            and node leaf weight
        nodes = [
            (tree_root,
             x_train.copy(),
             y_train.copy(),
             0.0)
        ]
        nb_nodes = 0
        real_depth = 0
        # Add node to tree using bfs
        while nodes:
```

```python
        node, node_x, node_y, prev_w = nodes.pop(
            0)
        node_x[
            'pred'] = self.predict(
                node_x)
        split_column = self._pick_columns(
            x_train.columns,
            node_x
        ) # XGBoost use a smarter heuristic here
        if split_column:
          cols = x_train.columns.tolist(
          )
          while cols:
            split_column = self._pick_columns(
                cols, node_x
            ) # XGBoost use a smarter heuristic here
            if not split_column:
              break
            best_split, split_value, left_w, right_w = \
                self._find_best_split(
                split_column,
                node_x,
                node_y,
                nb_nodes)
            if best_split != -1:
              break
            else:
              cols.remove(
                  split_column
              )
          if best_split != -1 and node.depth < self.\
              max_depth:
            self._add_child_nodes(
                node, nodes,
                node_x,
                node_y,
                split_value,
                split_column,
                node_count,
                left_w,
                right_w,
                prev_w)
          node_count += 2
          real_depth += 1
        nb_nodes += 1
        if nb_nodes >= 2**self.max_depth - 1:
          break
```

It starts by defining base_score, which defines the basic prediction, and which will be refined by the decision trees. It is calculated by assigning a value that is a rough but reasonable prediction, in this case, the average of the values to be predicted. It would also be possible to use the median.

The code then iterates over the list of root nodes constituting the set of decision trees created during the initialization of the class. For each root, the nodes list is initialized with the root node and the two training datasets. As long as this list is not empty, the top node of the list is retrieved.

A prediction is then made, based on the current decision set. It is this prediction that will be corrected with the new node added at this stage.

The column on which the new node will base its decision is retrieved by _pick_columns, which picks one at random. The choice of the value used as the decision threshold is made by brute force. This is what the _find_best_split method does, and how it works will be explained in a few lines.

Once the best criterion has been defined, the new node and its children are added to the current tree and to the nodes list thanks to _add_child_nodes.

Finally, if the depth reached with the addition of these nodes equals the maximum depth set for the trees, then the iterations stop.

The search for the best decision threshold, which will split the training dataset associated with the current node into two, is performed by _find_best_split using a brute force approach:

Listing 3.15: train_ensemble_tree.py

```python
def _find_best_split(
    self, col_name, node_x,
    node_y, nb_nodes):
    """

    Compute best split
    """

    x_sorted = node_x.sort_values(
        by=col_name)
    y_sorted = node_y[
        x_sorted.index]
    current_gain, _ = self._gain_and_weight(
        x_sorted, node_y,
        nb_nodes)
    gain = 0.0
    best_split = -1
    split_value, best_left_w, best_right_w = None, None
        , None
    for split_idx in range(
        1, x_sorted.shape[0]):
        # skip equal value
        if split_idx < x_sorted.shape[
            0] - 1:
```

```python
    if x_sorted.iloc[split_idx][
        col_name] == x_sorted.iloc[
            split_idx +
            1][col_name]:
        continue
    left_data = x_sorted.iloc[:
                        split_idx]
    right_data = x_sorted.iloc[
        split_idx:]
    left_y = y_sorted.iloc[:
                        split_idx]
    right_y = y_sorted.iloc[
        split_idx:]
    left_gain, left_w = self._gain_and_weight(
        left_data, left_y,
        nb_nodes)
    right_gain, right_w = self._gain_and_weight(
        right_data, right_y,
        nb_nodes)
    if current_gain - (
        left_gain +
        right_gain) > gain:
        gain = current_gain - (
            left_gain +
            right_gain)
        best_split = split_idx
        split_value = x_sorted[
            col_name].iloc[
                split_idx]
        best_left_w = left_w
        best_right_w = right_w
return best_split, split_value,
        best_left_w, best_right_w
```

For this purpose, training data is sorted in ascending order according to the chosen column. As long as two consecutive elements of the table are the same, the index is incremented, to find the position where the value changes.

The gain is then calculated according to the formula given in the mathematical foundation's section:

Listing 3.16: train_ensemble_tree.py

```python
def _gain_and_weight(
    self, x_train, y_train,
    nb_nodes):
    """
    Compute gain and leaf weight using automatic
        differentiation
    """

    pred = x_train[
        'pred'].values
```

```
    G_i = self.grad(
        pred,
        y_train.values).sum()
    H_i = self.hessian(
        pred,
        y_train.values).sum()
    return -0.5 * G_i * G_i / (
        H_i + self.lbda
    ) + self.gamma * nb_nodes, -G_i / (
        H_i + self.lbda)
```

The code then iterates by moving through the sorted data from
left to right and calculating the gain in the left and right nodes. If
the resulting gains are greater than the previous gain, the separation threshold is updated with this new value.

The decision generating the best gain is retained.


**Example**

Using this DecisionEnsemble class, it is now possible to train our
model on the training dataset and on the values to be predicted.
The loss function that will be used is the squared error. It is defined
by the lines below:

Listing 3.17: train_ensemble_tree.py

```
def squared_error(y_pred,
                  y_true):
    diff = y_true - y_pred
    return jnp.dot(diff, diff.T)
```

- the Jax library NumPy, through the alias jnp, is used here
to obtain the sum of the square of the differences. This ensures
that it is possible to use automatic differentiation to compute the
gradient and the hessian of this error.

The chosen training dataset contains a single predictor A, for
which the same value has to be predicted. It is defined by the
following variables:

Listing 3.18: train_ensemble_tree.py

```
x_train = pd.DataFrame({
    "A": [
        3.0, 2.0, 1.0, 4.0,
        5.0, 6.0, 7.0
    ]
})
y_train = pd.DataFrame({
    "Y": [
        3.0, 2.0, 1.0, 4.0,
        5.0, 6.0, 7.0
```

```
    ]
})
```

The function to be learned is therefore simply the identity function.

The first model constructed will attempt to learn this relationship with a single tree and a maximum depth of 3:

```
tree = DecisionEnsemble(squared_error, 1, 3)
```

Training is done by invoking the fit method:

```
tree.fit(x_train, y_train['Y'])
```

The model thus constructed can be tested by making a prediction:

```
pred = tree.predict(pd.DataFrame({'A': [1., 2., 3., 4.,
    5., 6., 7.]}))
print(pred) #-> [1. 2. 3. 4. 5. 6. 7.]
```

Which gives the expected result.

The figure below shows the resulting set of decision trees:

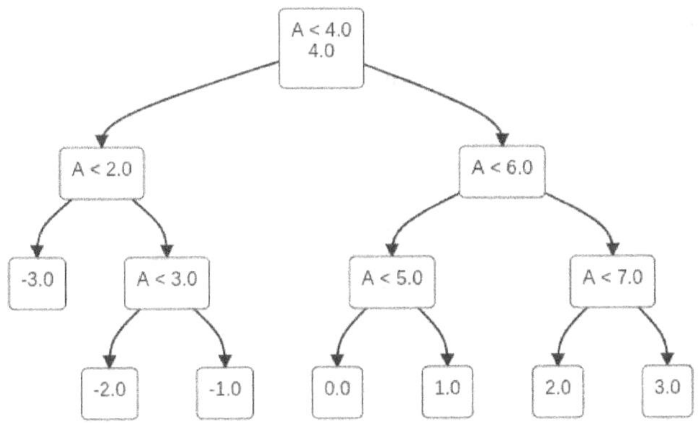


It is easy to check by hand that the tree gives the right values. With a more complex model, consisting of 2 trees with a maximum depth of 3, the result is also the expected one:

```
tree = DecisionEnsemble(squared_error, 2, 3)
tree.fit(x_train, y_train['Y'])
pred = tree.predict(pd.DataFrame({'A': [1., 2., 3., 4.,
    5., 6., 7.]}))
print(pred) #-> [1. 2. 3. 4. 5. 6. 7.]
```

Since the maximum depth allows a complete classification of the training data, the second tree is not useful, as shown by the learned tree set :

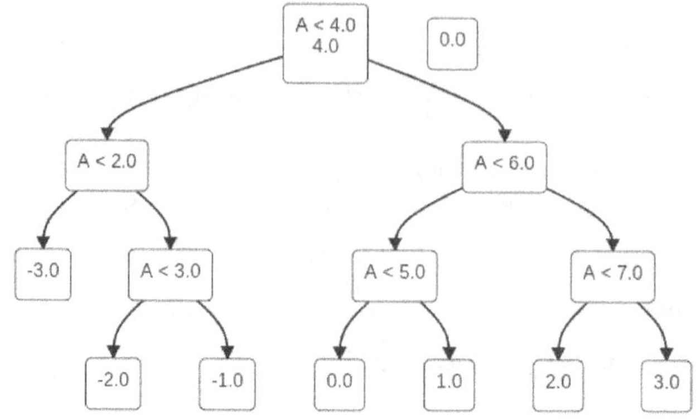

This second tree contains only a root with zero weight. If, on
the other hand, the depth of the trees to be used cannot exceed 2,
then in this case a minimum of 4 trees is necessary:

```
tree = DecisionEnsemble(squared_error, 4, 2)
tree.fit(x_train, y_train['Y'])
pred = tree.predict(pd.DataFrame({'A': [1., 2., 3., 4.,
    5., 6., 7.]}))
print(pred) # -> [1.  2.  3.  4.  5.  5.9999995 7.  ]
```

The generated tree set contains the following 4 trees:

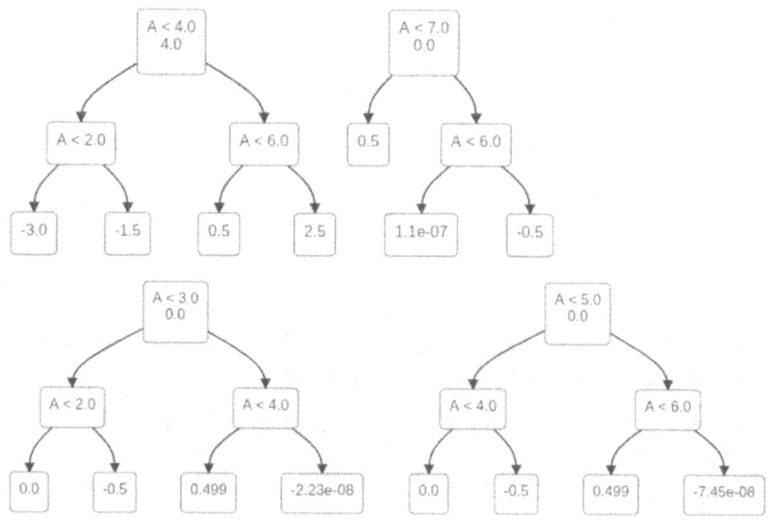

Finally, this last example is based on a more complex dataset:

```
x_train = pd.DataFrame({'A': [1.0, 2.0, 3.0, 4.0, 5.0,
    6.0, 7.0,
```

```
                              1.0, 2.0, 3.0, 4.0, 5.0,
                                 6.0, 7.0,],
                   'B': [0.0, 0.0, 0.0, 0.0, 0.0,
                         0.0, 0.0,
                           1.0, 1.0, 1.0, 1.0, 1.0,
                              1.0, 1.0,]})
y_train = pd.DataFrame({"Y" : [1.0, 2.0, 3.0, 4.0, 5.0,
    6.0, 7.0,
                                1.5, 2.5, 3.5, 4.5, 5.5,
                                   6.5, 7.5]})
For which a minimum depth of 6 is required when only
    one tree is used:
tree = DecisionEnsemble(squared_error, 1, 6)
tree.fit(x_train, y_train['Y'])
pred = tree.predict(pd.DataFrame({'A': [1., 2., 3., 4.,
    5., 6., 7.],
                        'B': [0., 1., 0., 1.,
                           0., 1., 0.]}))
print(pred) #-> [1.  2.5 3.  4.5 5.  6.5 7.  ]
```

The decision tree constructed to minimize the error is quite
complex:

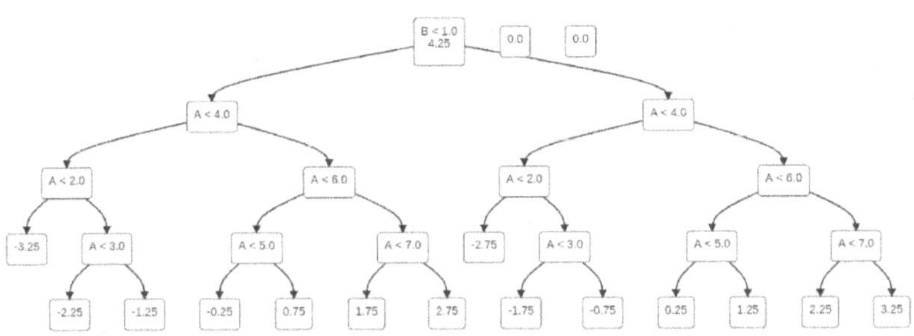

## 3.3.4  Regularisation

The previous section presented a minimal code for generating sets
of decision trees minimizing an error with respect to target data.
This new section will focus on regularisation, a key element to
control the structure of the generated trees, and ensure that the
models do not suffer from overfitting.

> ☞ In mathematics, regularisation consists in smoothing a continuous function, to make it derivable. The same principle can be found in physics, where it is applied to mathematical laws modeling physical behavior. The aim is then to make singularities disappear.
>
> This principle will be discussed in more detail in the chapter on the proper use of objective functions.

## On learning and generalization

The problem with ensemble methods and decision trees is that they are flexible enough to capture the structure of a data set in a very fine-grained way, provided that sufficient depth and trees are allowed.

This ability to adapt, coupled with the imprecision and noise of real data, leads to overfitting. That is, the model has conformed too much to variations in the training data, including those resulting from simple measurement errors or special cases.

This overfitting impairs the model's ability to generalize: when it is confronted with new data, which are not part of the training dataset, it will try to reproduce too finely what it has learned, without generalizing to these new data.

The following code illustrates this in the simple case where a strictly negative value is given the label -1 and any positive or zero value is given the label +1. The expected result is a tree with a single node and two leaves, testing for the positivity of the input number.

```python
# train_ensemble_regularisation.py
x_train = pd.DataFrame({"A" : [-3.0, -2.0, -1.0, 0.0,
    1.0, 2.0, 3.0]})
y_train = pd.DataFrame({"Y" : [-1, -1, -1, 1.0, 1.0,
    1.0, 1.0]})

tree = DecisionEnsemble(squared_error, 1, 6)
tree.fit(x_train, y_train['Y'])
pred = tree.predict(pd.DataFrame({'A': [-3.0, -2.0,
    -1.0, 0.0, 1.0, 2.0, 3.0]}))
print(pred) #-> [-1.  -1.  -1.  1.  1.  1.  1.]

# overfitting
y_train = pd.DataFrame({"Y" : [-1, -1, -1, 1.0, 1.0,
    1.0, 1.0]})
y_train['Y'] = y_train['Y'] + np.random.normal(0, .1,
    y_train.shape[0])

tree = DecisionEnsemble(squared_error, 1, 6)
```

```python
tree.fit(x_train, y_train['Y'])
pred = tree.predict(pd.DataFrame({'A': [-3.0, -2.0,
    -1.0, 0.0, 1.0, 2.0, 3.0]}))
print(pred) #-> [-0.9040482 -0.9865432 -0.99615836
    1.0572047 0.8786878 0.7685069 0.9598383 ]

# regularization
tree = DecisionEnsemble(squared_error, 1, 6, gamma=1)
tree.fit(x_train, y_train['Y'])
pred = tree.predict(pd.DataFrame({'A': [-3.0, -2.0,
    -1.0, 0.0, 1.0, 2.0, 3.0]}))
print(pred) #-> [-0.96225 -0.96225 -0.96225 0.9160595
    0.9160595 0.9160595 0.9160595]
```

The first two lines create perfect training data, with no measurement error or variability.

A first model is trained on this data, with sufficient depth to
allow overfitting. The prediction is exactly as expected.

A second model is then trained, but this time on noisy data.
Again, the model accurately predicted the values present in the
training dataset. This is shown in the figure below. It has therefore
captured the noise present in the data: this is a case of overfitting.

A third and final model is trained, again on the noisy data, but
using the gamma regularisation parameter. As seen in the section
on the mathematical foundations of gradient boosting, the latter
is used to penalize the construction of trees with too many leaves.
It thus avoids having trees that are too deep, a sign of overfitting.
This time, the model predicts only two values: one for strictly
negative numbers, and one for positive or zero numbers.

The plot below graphically represents the results obtained by
this listing:

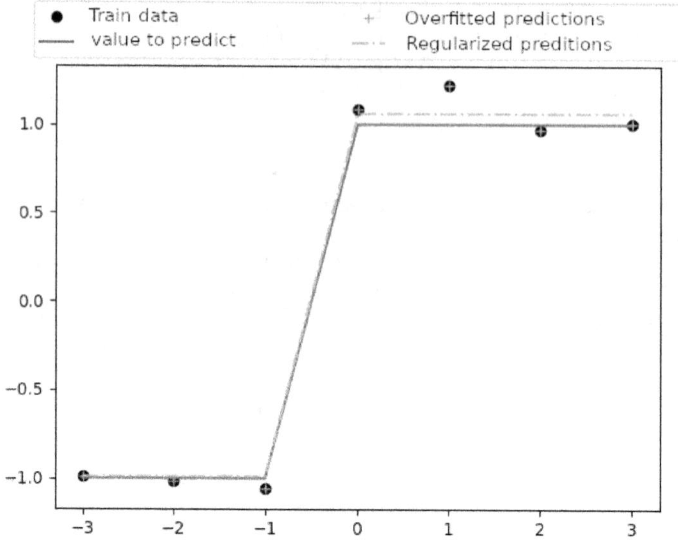

The over-learned model has captured too much variability.

This other plot shows the predictions of the over-trained and regularised models when confronted with data outside the training dataset:

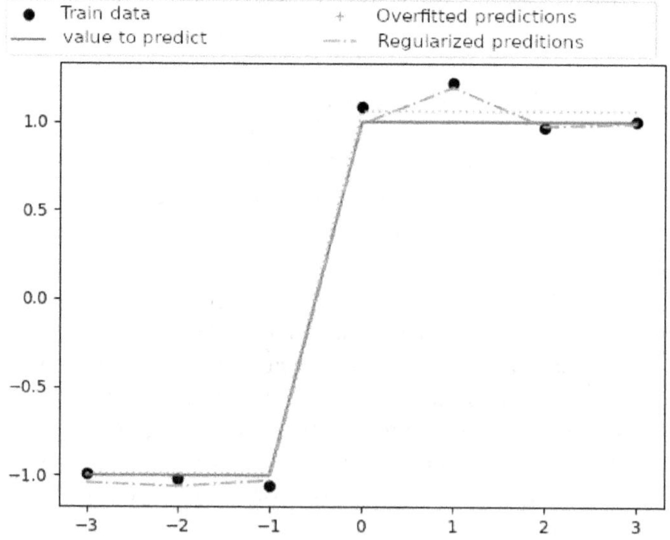

Again, the regularised model gives better results.

> ☞ These last two graphs highlight another way of looking at the problem of overfitting and generalization: the bias-variance tradeoff. Either the model chosen is simple but still biased, as is the case for the regularised model. Or the model captures the variance and is unbiased with respect to the data, but in this case, it is overlearned.

It is also instructive to look at the structure of the trees generated in the three cases. This is ultimately the most important point, which ensures that our model has understood the nature of the problem.

The first one, learned on the perfect data, has a simple structure:

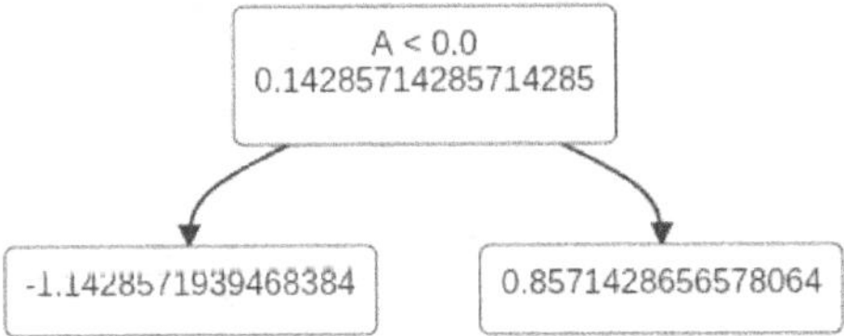


The weight attached to the first node is the base score, base_score. Summed with the weights of each node, the prediction is indeed -1 or A depending on the sign of A.

The second, when confronted with noisy data without activation of the regularisation, is artificially complex:

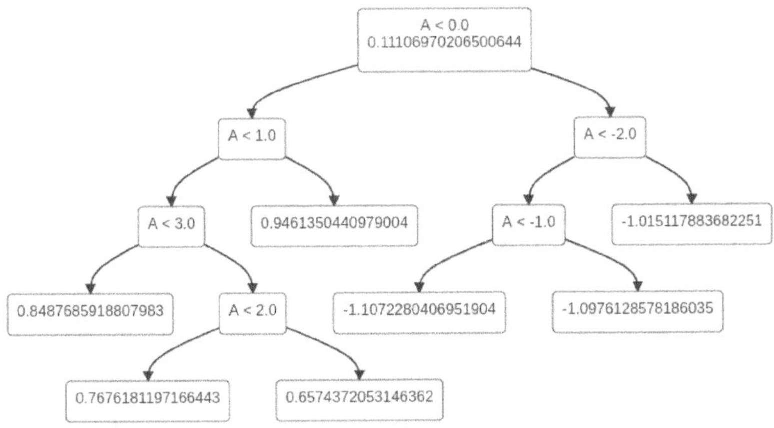


Even if its error on the training data is almost zero, it is unnecessarily overcomplicated, and above all, it has not understood the simply binary nature of the dataset.

Finally, the third, for which regularisation has been activated, finds a structure adapted to the problem:

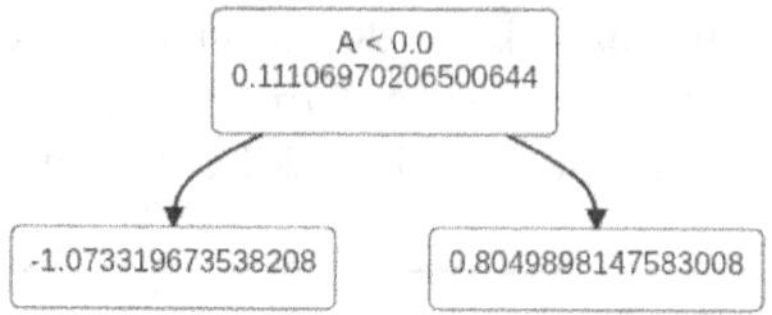


The error is certainly more marked than in the over-learned case, but the structure of the dataset is well identified by the model: the generated tree offers two possibilities of prediction.

# Chapter 4

# Train a model efficiently

## 4.1 Train effectively

The theory, the mathematical foundations, and the implementation of Gradient Boosting methods have been presented in the previous chapter, it is time to move on to practice.

To do so, we will describe in this chapter the conditions to be respected to ensure an efficient training, which allows the production of accurate and correctly generalizing models.

After a quick overview of the main steps in training a model, a second section will deal in detail with the preparation of the data, their cleaning and enrichment, and the construction of the training and evaluation datasets.

The third section will briefly present the principles of training itself, while the fourth section will dive into the details of the different metrics used to evaluate the quality of a regression or classification model.

The fifth section will deal with the problem of overfitting, its detection, and the levers offered by Gradient Boosting methods to avoid it.

Finally, some practical cases from open-source data will be studied.

### 4.1.1 Overall approach

Before diving into the arcana of training, it is important to give an overview of the major steps involved. The diagram below gives a synthetic view:

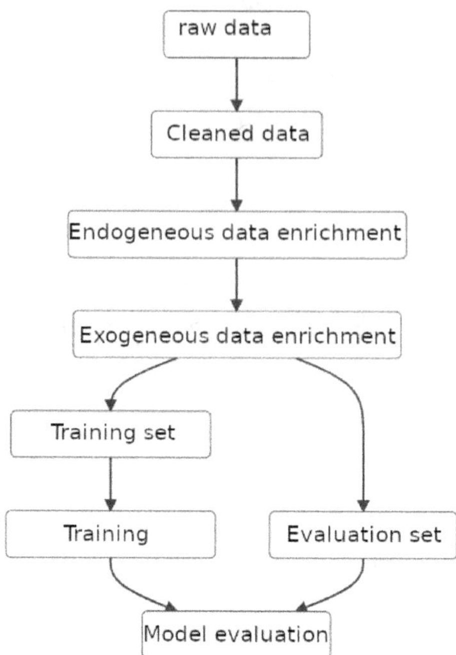


Starting from the raw data, which are successively cleaned and enriched endogenously and exogenously, training is done on a subset of the data, while the remaining data are put aside for future evaluation.

☞ It is crucial to distinguish between test datasets and evaluation datasets. Test datasets are used during training, to evaluate the learning progress.

Evaluation datasets are used only after the model has been built, to ensure the generalizability of the model.

It is imperative that these two types of datasets, test, and validation, be well partitioned, to avoid any bias during the evaluation.

## 4.2    Data preparation

The key element in training a model is the data. No matter how complex or sophisticated a model is if the data available are not representative of the problem, are not rich enough, or are not numerous enough, then the quality of the prediction will not be satisfactory.

As highlighted in the diagram above, this phase must be done before the construction of the training and evaluation datasets, while taking care not to contaminate the evaluation dataset by leaking data.

### 4.2.1 Data Enrichment

The richness of a corpus of data lies in the presence of numerous characteristics, or features, which offer a vision from several angles of the problem.

In the context of social-economic analyses, the more qualified the population studied is and through numerous indicators, the more precise the modesl built will be. Income, lifestyle, diet, level of education, leisure, sleep time, family size, relationship with ancestors and descendants, assets... all information deserves to be collected.

In this example, the data enriching the corpus are external. It is therefore exogenous data.

Another way to enrich a dataset is to augment it with endogenous data.

These are additional features that are built not by looking outward, but rather by staying within the existing data and reworking it.

Time series are a good example. The raw signal that constitutes them is generally derived from the sampling at a given frequency of measurements from a sensor. This type of signal contains intrinsically a lot of information, but it must be extracted. Numerous treatments can be applied such as a Fourier transform, a wavelet decomposition, a calculation of energy, amplitude, or other convolutions,... all of which improve the raw data and increase the performance of a model.

### 4.2.2 Data volume

This is the first criterion to consider. The more complex the system to be modeled, the more data will be needed to capture the complexity. For example, if the task at hand is to classify an image into one of 1000 categories, at least 1000 data samples are required.

The volume of data is also to be put in relation to the hyperparameters, which preside over the construction of the decision tree ensemble. If it is for example the fruit of the assembly of 100 trees of depth 4, it takes at least $100 * 4^2 = 1600$ different data samples to feed the 1600 leaves of these trees.

The number of rows is not the only criterion to consider when it comes to volume. The number of columns and the cardinality of the single elements within a column must also be taken into account.

It is impossible for example to classify images in 1000 categories with only 2 columns each containing 2 distinct values. Even if the training dataset contains millions of rows, there will always be only 2x2 = 4 different types of images.

### 4.2.3   Data cleansing

One phase that should not be overlooked is data cleansing. Even though progress in data collection and storage has been made, the data scientist is still confronted with three main types of data cleansing: poorly formatted data, outliers, and inconsistent data.

Badly formatted data is annoying to process but can be easily identified and corrected. For example, there are format problems in CSV files. It is impossible to process data unless it is in the correct format.

Outliers are more easily identified. They are for example temperatures below absolute zero, or speeds exceeding the speed of light. Some business rules allow us to identify them. The question then arises as to what to do with them: should they be corrected or deleted? The answer is often to be found in the volume and representativeness of the available data. If they are numerous, it is more prudent to discard them. If the dataset is poor, it may be worthwhile to try to correct them.

Finally, inconsistent data are the most difficult to recognize. Taken individually, each feature may seem correct, but a more global analysis often highlights these inconsistencies. In this case, it is necessary to rely on the man of the art to identify and treat them.

### 4.2.4   Data completeness

Another topic that is quite similar to cleaning is missing data. It often happens that for a sample of data, not all characteristics are present.

In this case, two alternatives are possible, again depending on the amount of data available: either these data rows are simply deleted, or the missing data are filled with default values.

Several strategies can be used to determine the value to be used as a substitute: it can be a constant, an average, a median, or the most frequent category, ... It is up to the Data Scientist to judge the most relevant one.

### 4.2.5 Integration of categorical data

The essence of how decision trees work is to partition the data in such a way as to apply specific corrections to each partition. This partitioning is based on the data of a given characteristic, by determining the optimal split threshold.

This implies that it is possible to order the stored values of a feature. If the values are numerical, this is not a problem. On the other hand, if the data are categorical, this ordering relation does not exist.

To feed a decision tree model, depending on the libraries used, it will be necessary to apply preprocessing to these data.

> ☞ CatBoost is an implementation of Gradient Boosting methods for decision trees that works directly on categorical data. No preprocessing is required.

Several solutions are applicable to achieve this conversion. The best known is One Hot Encoding, which proceeds by creating a column for each category. If a row of data contains a given category, then the new column associated with it will contain a 1, while the other columns will remain at 0.

This can also be more advanced methods like glmm encoding.

The table below illustrates this mechanism:

| Line | Color | Red | Green | BLue |
|------|-------|-----|-------|------|
| 1 | Red | 1 | 0 | 0 |
| 2 | Green | 0 | 1 | 0 |
| 3 | Blue | 0 | 0 | 1 |

The major drawback of this method is that it introduces as many columns as there are different categories. In the example above, three colors have generated three additional columns.

As soon as the number of categories exceeds 100, this can become problematic regarding computation time.

It is then necessary to turn to other solutions, such as Target Encoding or GLMM Encoding, which will allow the addition of only one column.

### 4.2.6 Training dataset

Building the training dataset, once the data has been pre-processed as we have just seen, is quite simple. This is usually done as a hollowing out of the evaluation dataset: the training dataset usually contains the remaining data.

This is to be qualified, however, by not forgetting that this dataset must be representative of the problem and that it is therefore necessary to ensure that it is balanced. The data collected may contain more of this or that type of case. It is therefore necessary in this case to ensure representativeness and balance.

### 4.2.7   Evaluation dataset

**Role of the evaluation dataset**

The other key element when building a model is the evaluation dataset. It is crucial because it will allow us to judge the quality of the model by subjecting it to data that it has never encountered. This phase evaluates the model's ability to generalize.

This dataset must therefore be carefully constructed to be sufficiently representative of the problem being tested. The difficulty that generally emerges during its creation is that it cannot be too large, as all the data that are found in the evaluation dataset are data that will not benefit the training.

> ☞ There is a pitfall to be avoided absolutely when setting up the evaluation dataset: it is imperative to ensure that during the data enrichment phase, particularly endogenous, there has been no data leakage between the training dataset and the evaluation dataset.
>
> This would bias the model and its evaluation!

The size of this dataset, as a proportion of the initial data, is generally in the order of 10 to 30%.

**Importance of a good partitionning**

The assembly of the evaluation dataset must be done meticulously so that it is a reduced but complete version of the problem under consideration.

If, for example, the task to perform is a classification, but only 30% of the classes of the problem are present in the evaluation dataset, then the evaluation of the quality of the model will be partial.

In addition, not only must each class be represented, but also in a homogeneous manner. If one or more classes were to take precedence over the others, then the evaluation of the model would again be biased against these classes.

The same is true for regression problems, where the distribution of each feature must be similar to that of the training dataset.

## 4.3 Training

The training phase itself takes place after the data pre-processing and training dataset creation phases. I.e. the model will be fitted using the data. Concretely speaking, this means that the parameters of the model will be learned. In the case of Decision Trees, we are speaking of the leaves weights and node decision criteria.

### 4.3.1 Choice of Hyper Parameters

The major difficulty at this stage is to identify the optimal hyperparameters for the considered problem. The Hyper Parameters Tuning chapter will go into detail on this crucial step.

### 4.3.2 Choice of the objective

The chapter on the operation of Gradient Boosting methods showed that the entire Gradient Boosting method is based on an objective function. From the identification of the decision criteria for each node to the value of the leaf weights, everything is derived from this function through its Gradient and its Hessian.

Choosing the right objective function is therefore absolutely crucial, starting by choosing one that is adapted to the use case: regression or classification.

In the case of regression, the choice of the objective function, or loss function depending on the implementation, is often reduced to the squared_error.

> ☞ Objective functions based on the squared error have interesting properties, as shown in the chapter on the operation of Gradient Boosting methods.
>
> In particular, without regularization, the optimal value computed for the leaf weights is none other than the average of the error.

In the case of classification, depending on the nature of the classification, the objective function is either the logistic function in the binary case or the softmax function in the multi-class case.

The choice of the logistic function is motivated by the fact that, outside the transition zone, it gives two values: 0 or 1. Hence its use for binary classification.

The softmax function, on the other hand, is multi-valued, i.e. it calculates not a scalar but a vector. It is constructed in such a way that in the resulting vector, the most probable class has a value close to 1 while the others tend towards zero. It is a generalization of the logistic function for n values.

> ☞ As reminded in the chapter on the functioning of Gradient Boosting methods, the objective function must be derivable twice. This limits the field of possibilities.
>
> The chapter dedicated to the good use of objective functions will come back in detail on the possibilities offered by the regularization of initially non-derivable functions such as the Mean Absolute Error (MAE).

## 4.4  Metrics

Once the model has been trained, the quality of the generated model must be assessed. To do this, we need to calculate metrics that will quantify the quality of the prediction made versus the real values.

> ☞ It is important to distinguish between metrics, used for evaluation, and objective functions, used for training.
>
> They do not have the same role or the same mathematical properties.

These metrics are calculated at two points: during training, ideally using the Cross Validation method to which we will return later, and during evaluation.

### 4.4.1  Role of metrics

This section presents the most commonly used metrics for estimating the value of a model. It is important to keep in mind that it is essential not to limit oneself to a single metric but to consider several to have an global overview of the quality of the model.

Metrics, like objective functions, rely on the error for their calculations, because it is the error, i.e. the difference between reality and the predicted values, that allows us to gauge the quality of a model, both for regression and for classification.

Metrics are a way of aggregating these errors, so that you can form an overall opinion of performance, without having to consider them line by line.

### 4.4.2  Scope of metrics calculation

It is important to understand that these metrics can be calculated on both the training and evaluation datasets. The metrics evaluated on these two perimeters must be analyzed jointly. In particular, the quality of a model cannot be judged solely based on metrics on the training dataset. This would run the risk of encouraging overfitting, as will be detailed in the next section.

It is therefore essential to calculate these metrics on these two datasets.

### 4.4.3   Metrics for regression

**Mean Absolute Error**

The first thing that comes to the mind of the apprentice Data Scientist, when he wants to evaluate the performance of his first regression model, is simply, to sum up, the errors for each prediction, or even better to average them.

The problem with this approach is that we sum positive and negative errors indistinctly. However, if the model is balanced, and if over- and under-prediction compensate each other, then the overall error, in sum or in average, can be zero, giving the false impression of a good model. This is obviously not the case.

To overcome this problem, we simply need to look at the absolute value of the errors, which is conventionally averaged to provide an overall indicator.

This is the Mean Absolute Error (MAE). It gives an overview of the number of units that the model is wrong on average, regardless of over or under-prediction.

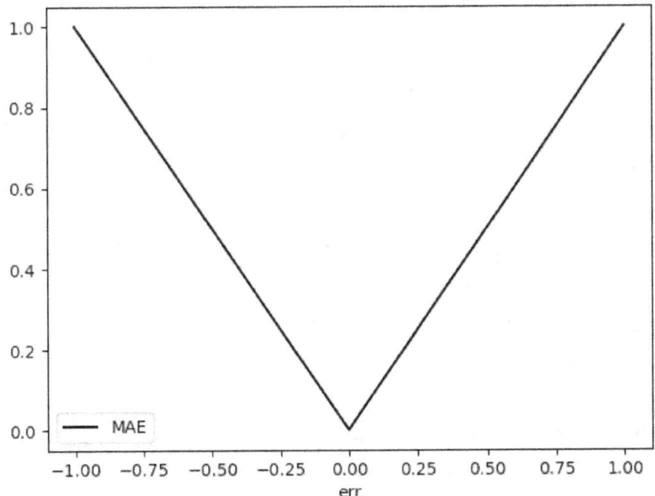

> ☞ As the above curve shows, the MAE is not derivable (there is a discontinuity in the derivative at zero), and therefore cannot be used as an objective function.

One of the advantages of this metric, apart from its intelligibility, is that it is robust to outliers. It will therefore not be impacted too brutally by a few points that have significant errors.

The following listing shows how to calculate it:

```python
import numpy as np

def MAE(y_true, y_pred):
    err = y_true - y_pred
    mae = np.mean(abs(err))
    return mae

y_true = np.array([1, 2, 3, 4])
y_pred = np.array([1.1, 1.9, 2.7, 4.1])
print(MAE(y_true, y_pred))
# -> 0.1499
```

## Mean Absolute Percentage Error

The second piece of information that the data scientist commonly wants is a percentage idea of the accuracy of the model.

For this, he can use a variation of the MAE, the Mean Absolute Percentage Error (MAPE).

This time it gives an idea of the error, but as a percentage, which allows a more immediate understanding of the quality of a model.

However, it suffers from an intrinsic bias, for small values: an error of one unit with respect to a real value of 1 will generate a percentage error of 100%.

In the didactic case where two predictions would be made, one with a value of 2 for a reality of 1, and the other with a value of 9 for a reality of 10, the overall MAPE would be 55% which would give a poor estimate of the model.

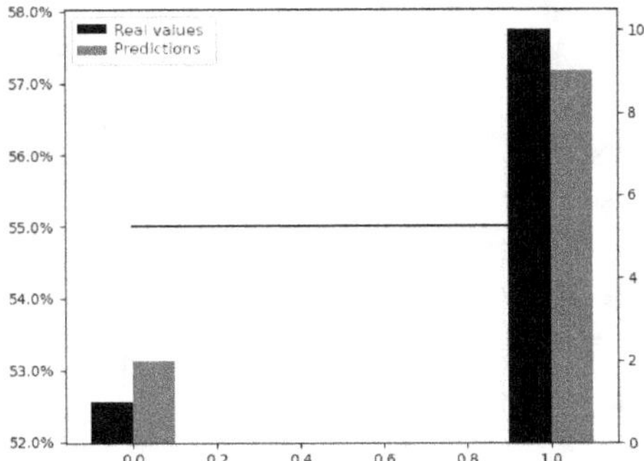


Including the MAE in the analysis would ensure a more relevant scoring, as the MAE would be 1.

MAPE is implemented as follows:

```python
import numpy as np

def MAPE(y_true, y_pred):
    err = y_true - y_pred
    mape = np.mean(abs(err) / y_true)
    return mape

y_true = np.array([1, 2, 3, 4])
y_pred = np.array([1.1, 1.9, 2.7, 4.1])
print(MAPE(y_true, y_pred))
# -> 0.0687
```

This code also highlights that MAPE cannot be computed if one of the true values is zero, because this would imply a division by 0.

In this case, it is possible to turn to the SMAPE, which is a symmetrical version.

**Mean Squared Error**

Another way to get around the problem of offsetting negative errors with positive errors, which irreparably biases the estimate, is to use the square of the error instead of the absolute value.

As with the MAE, an average is applied to aggregate the errors and get an overall picture of performance.

The interest of this measure is that it is very close to the function regularly used as a target for Gradient Boosting: the squared error.

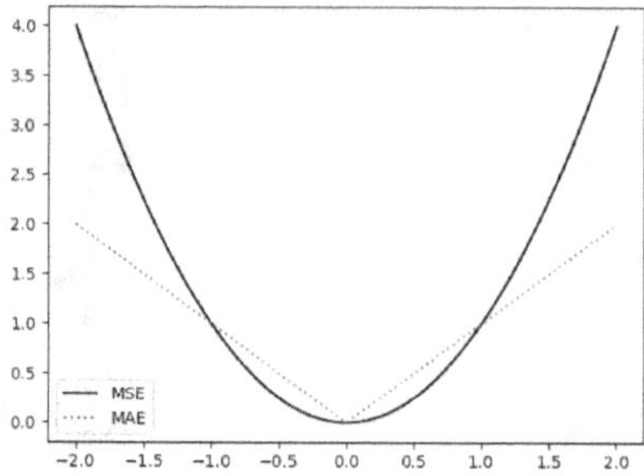

> ☞ Unlike the MAE, the MSE is very sensitive to outliers. Some predictions with a large error can affect it significantly because their error is squared before being averaged.

Its implementation is trivial:

```python
import numpy as np

def MSE(y_true, y_pred):
    err = y_true - y_pred
    mse = np.mean(err.dot(err))
    return mse

y_true = np.array([1, 2, 3, 4])
y_pred = np.array([1.1, 1.9, 2.7, 4.1])
print(MSE(y_true, y_pred))
# -> 0.119
```

## RMSE

The Root Meas Squared Error, the RMSE, is very similar to the MSE. It just applies the square root function to the MSE, to provide a value of the same dimension as the original error, not a squared dimension.

It is coded in a very similar way to the IEM, simply using the square root function sqrt :

```python
import numpy as np
import math

def RMSE(y_true, y_pred):
    err = y_true - y_pred
    rmse = math.sqrt(np.mean(err.dot(err)))
    return rmse
```

```python
y_true = np.array([1, 2, 3, 4])
y_pred = np.array([1.1, 1.9, 2.7, 4.1])
print(RMSE(y_true, y_pred))
# -> 0.346
```

## Coefficient of determination: $R^2$

The metrics presented up to this point sought to quantify the accuracy of the predictions, and thus of the model. Roughly speaking, a low value indicated that the model was pretty accurate, while a high value indicated an unreliable model.

The purpose of the coefficient of determination is different: it does not qualify the accuracy of the model, but its ability to capture the complexity of the problem under study. In other words, this coefficient quantifies the explanatory value of the model.

It is an indicator of how much of the variance in the data being studied is captured by the model. Its value can be negative but never exceeds 1.

When it is 1, it indicates that all variability in the data is explained by the model.

If it is 0, as suggested by the code below, this indicates that the model does not do better than a prediction that would simply be the average.

```python
import NumPy as np
import math

def R2(y_true, y_pred):
    err = y_true - y_pred
    y_true_mean = np.mean(y_true)
    mean_err = y_true - y_true_mean
    r2 = 1.0 - np.sum(err.dot(err)) / np.sum(mean_err.
        dot(mean_err))
    return r2

y_true = np.array([1, 2, 3, 4])
y_pred = np.array([1.1, 1.9, 2.7, 4.1])
y_mean = np.array([2.5] * 4)
print(R2(y_true, y_pred))
# -> 0.976
print(R2(y_true, y_mean))
# -> 0.346
```

## Simple reference model

One discipline that a data scientist should always follow is to systematically build a simple model for comparison.

Indeed, there is no point in developing a hyper-complex model as long as it is not possible to evaluate its gain compared to a basic model.

A good candidate for this model is an average model, which consist, at the finest possible resolution, in offering as a prediction the average at that resolution.

For example, in the case of a dataset for which the selling price of a house should be predicted according to its characteristics, a first reference model would simply be based on the average price per squared meters.

The set of metrics presented above is then applied to the model resulting from the training of decision trees with the Gradient Boosting method and the reference model, then compared.


### 4.4.4   Metrics for classification

In a classification exercise, the evaluation of the quality of a prediction is more binary than in the case of prediction: either the correct class has been assigned to the sample, or not. It is a binary problem.

The metrics implemented reflect this binary nature and are essentially variations in the ratio between the number of correct and incorrect classifications.


**Precision**

The first metric that can be used is the ratio between the number of correct classifications and the number of samples to be classified. A perfect classification generates a score of 1.0, while a completely wrong classification generates a score of 0.0.

The few lines of code below illustrate this metric using sklearn :

```python
from sklearn.metrics import accuracy_score

y_pred = [0, 1, 1, 2]
y_true = [0, 1, 2, 1]

print(accuracy_score(y_true, y_pred))
# -> 0.5
```

> ☞   There is a variant of this metric, the balanced_accuracy, which takes into account the frequency of each class, and weights the error by this frequency, to account for an imbalance in the data.

### False positives

Another simple metric is the number of false positives, which indicates how many samples were wrongly classified in one class when they belonged to another.

> ☞ In the case of multi-class classification, this score is to be calculated for a given class.

### False negatives

The number of false negatives measures the inverse effect of false positives, i.e. the case where another class has been assigned to a sample.

> ☞ In the case of multi-class classification, this score is to be calculated for a given class.

### Confusion matrix

The confusion matrix is an easy way to get a global view of the quality of a classifier.

Each row of this matrix concerns a given class. Each column corresponds to a class, and gives the number of elements of the class corresponding to that of the row, and classified in the class of the column.

An error-free classification will therefore give a purely diagonal matrix. Ideally, one should obtain a diagonal matrix, i.e. with values in the diagonal greater than the sum of the off-diagonal values.

The code below gives a more precise idea of this principle:

```python
from sklearn.metrics import confusion_matrix

y_pred = [0, 1, 1, 2]
y_true = [0, 1, 2, 1]

print(confusion_matrix(y_true, y_pred))
# -> [[1 0 0]
# [0 1 1]
# [0 1 0]]
```

Here, no errors were made for class 0, while class 1 was confused with class 2, and class 2 was never correctly identified.

**Accuracy**

Precision is another metric based on the notion of true and false positives. It is defined as the ratio of samples correctly assigned to a class to the total number of samples assigned to that class.

It is therefore equal to 1 when the classification is perfect and tends to zero when the classification deteriorates.

**Recall**

Recall is another metric to look at in conjunction with precision, this time based on the ratio of correctly labeled samples to the number of samples in that class.

Again, a ratio of 1.0 indicates a perfect classification, while a value below 1.0 highlights that the classifier has missed samples.

**F1-score**

Recall and classification are scores that are usually analyzed at the same time. It is therefore interesting to have a metric that combines them into a single term.

This is what the f1-score proposes, whose formula follows:

$$2 * \frac{precision \cdot recall}{precision + recall}$$

This formula can be rewritten in the following form, to show a form of harmonic mean:

$$\frac{2}{precision^{-1} + recall^{-1}}$$

### 4.4.5   Cross Validation

After this overview of the applicable metrics for evaluating the quality of a regression or classification model, it is interesting to specify how to compute them reliably in the training phase.

**Motivation for Cross Validation**

Indeed, these scores are only accurate if they are calculated on all the data. However, a part of this data is used for the training dataset, while the rest is used for the evaluation dataset. Their computation during the training phase, therefore, requires reducing the training dataset to extract a test dataset.

The evaluation of these metrics is therefore done on a sub-part, necessarily reduced, of the data initially available. There is therefore no guarantee that this test subset will be representative of the problem, and that the score will be characteristic of the quality of the model.

One solution could be to take a larger test dataset, but this would mean reducing the training dataset, which would not be beneficial.

## Principle of Cross Validation

To avoid this pitfall, i.e. to rely on an arbitrary and small test dataset, the Cross Validation method is often used. The principle of this method is to carry out several training sessions by splitting the initial training data into several pairs of training datasets/test datasets. As many trainings as train/test couples are performed, and the different metrics are calculated for each case.

In this way, the risk of having built a test dataset that is not representative of the problem is reduced, since it will be spread over several test datasets. The global metrics are then the average of the metrics calculated for each pair of training datasets/test datasets.

It remains to find a compromise between the number of pairs and the training time. Indeed, the greater the number of combinations tested, the more reliable the scores obtained, but the greater the computation time. On the other hand, in the extreme case of a single pair, the risk of a bad evaluation returns.

## Possible partitionning

There are many ways to build these training dataset/test dataset couples.

The most common method is the KFold method, which randomly divides the data into K groups, and randomly draws combinations of K-1 groups to form the training dataset. The remaining group is then used as the test dataset.

The following image illustrates this breakdown with a cross-validation number set to 4. The test dataset appears in light grey:

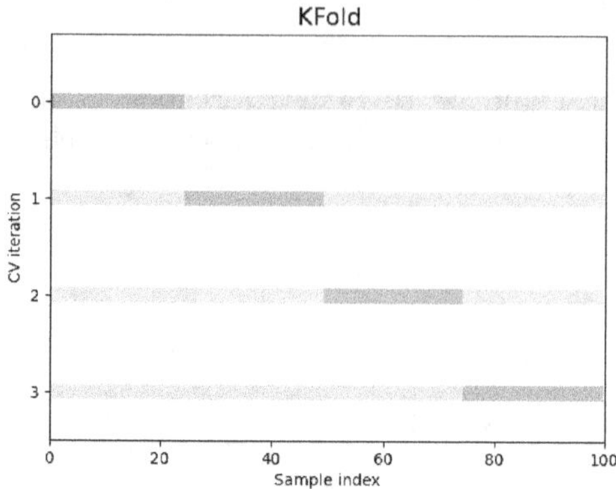



An alternative that deserves to be mentioned, and to which we will return a little later, is the TimeSeriesSplit method, applied to time series. The idea is to start from a dataset sorted by ascending date and to cut at the end K groups of data. Each of these groups is used as a test dataset, and the strictly previous data is used for training.

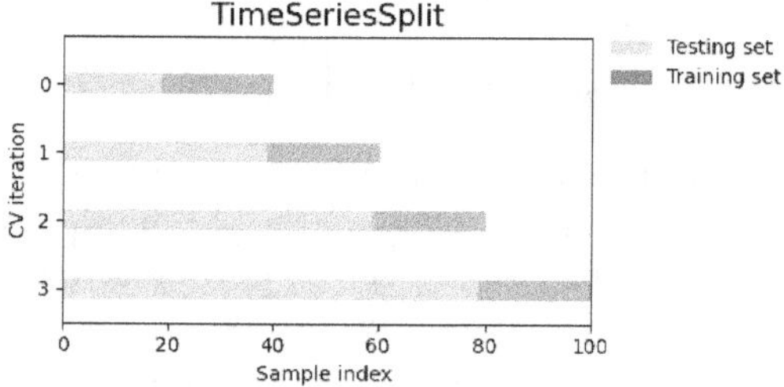



## 4.5   The trap of overfitting

### 4.5.1   Description

Models based on decision trees are very powerful. Provided they are allowed to develop freely, i.e. are not constrained in their number and depth, then they can conform precisely to the dataset on which they are trained.

In this case, they can generate very accurate predictions for every row in the training dataset. All the metrics that were scanned above, essentially error-based, will therefore be very good, if not ideal. The model will have overlearned.

An untrained data scientist would be delighted with these results and the excellence of his model. Unfortunately, the opposite is true: the model is overfitted, and will not deliver good results when presented with data that does not belong to the training dataset.

Its ability to generalize on unknown data will be limited and so will the interest of the model.

## 4.5.2 Detection

If the overall approach presented in the introduction to this chapter has been followed, identifying a case of overfitting is easy. The metrics obtained during training, even using Cross Validation, will be very good. On the contrary, they will be bad on the evaluation dataset.

The code below shows a case of overfitting on an artificial dataset, created by the make_classification method:

```python
# ch3_overfit.py
import numpy as np
from sklearn.datasets import make_classification
from sklearn.model_selection import train_test_split


from xgboost import XGBClassifier
import matplotlib.pyplot as plt

X, y = make_classification(n_samples=100,
                           n_informative=5,
                           n_classes=3,
                           random_state=5)

X_train, X_test, y_train, y_test = train_test_split(X,
    y, test_size=0.2, random_state=42)

eval_set = [(X_train, y_train), (X_test, y_test)]
model = XGBClassifier(use_label_encoder=False,
                      verbose=True,
                      num_class=3)

model.fit(X_train, y_train,
          eval_metric=['mlogloss'],
          eval_set=eval_set)
# [0] validation_0-mlogloss:0.80954
#     validation_1-mlogloss:0.91414
# [1] validation_0-mlogloss:0.61295
#     validation_1-mlogloss:0.80010
# [2] validation_0-mlogloss:0.46815
#     validation_1-mlogloss:0.72442
# [3] validation_0-mlogloss:0.36609
#     validation_1-mlogloss:0.66446
# [4] validation_0-mlogloss:0.29383
#     validation_1-mlogloss:0.64616
```

```
# [5] validation_0-mlogloss:0.23800
      validation_1-mlogloss:0.61983
# [6] validation_0-mlogloss:0.19832
      validation_1-mlogloss:0.59875
# [7] validation_0-mlogloss:0.16526
      validation_1-mlogloss:0.58952
# [8] validation_0-mlogloss:0.14131
      validation_1-mlogloss:0.57995
# [9] validation_0-mlogloss:0.12145
      validation_1-mlogloss:0.57413
# [10] validation_0-mlogloss:0.10602
      validation_1-mlogloss:0.58198
```

## Solutions

During the training, performed by calling the fit method, two datasets were provided for evaluation: the training dataset and the test dataset. At each iteration, the mlogloss metric is evaluated and displayed for these two datasets. Each iteration corresponds to the addition of a new tree.

By plotting these two errors as a function of the number of trees added, the phenomenon of overfitting appears clearly:

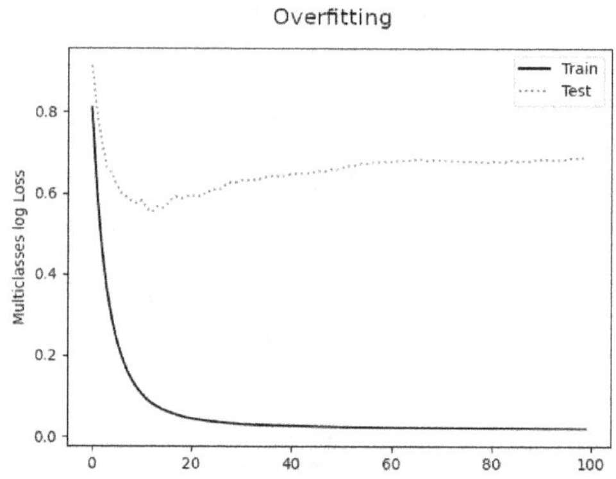


The best model, i.e. the one that generalizes the best, is reached for about 18 trees, while the one obtained in the end, involving 100 trees, underperforms on the test dataset. This is indeed an a case of overfitting.

Several solutions can be put in place to avoid this phenomenon of overfitting. The following sections detail them.

### Constraints on Hyper Parameters

The first is to force the generated models to remain simple by playing on the hyperparameters that govern their structure. A chapter is dedicated to them later in the book.

The two main ones to watch closely are the maximum depth of the tree and the number of estimators.

A maximum depth that is too large implies a number of leaves that, doubling at each new stage, may end up being equal to the number of rows in the training dataset. In this extreme case, each leaf then gives a value to be learned.

In the same way, too many estimators, i.e. decision trees, even with a limited depth, can stick too closely to the data to be learned.

## Regularization

Another way to achieve the same result, but in a more mathematically elegant and robust way, is to rely on the regularization parameters of the model. The chapter describing the theoretical operation of Gradient Boosting presented the parameters gamma and lambda, but there are others such as alpha.

Each implementation of Gradient Boosting for decision trees has its own. The general idea, which we will come back to in detail in the chapter on Hyper Parameters Tuning, is to control the construction of the structure of the tree set. This is done by allowing the addition of new nodes or new trees only under certain conditions.

## Sub-sampling

Overfitting arises from taking advantage of all the data available in the training data. Using only a subset of the data addresses the source of the problem and is effective.

To keep the benefit of using all the data and its representativeness, the different implementations of Gradient Boosting for decision trees such as XGBoost and CatBoost propose options that allow keeping only a certain percentage of the initial dataset, either by considering the rows or by considering the columns

This is a mechanism similar to the dropout used in deep neural networks.

## Early stopping

There is another mechanism to limit the complexity of models, and therefore the risk of overfitting. It is called early stopping.

The motivation for this method is simple: if adding new trees to the existing set does not bring any gain, there is no point in continuing to enrich the model any longer. We might as well stop prematurely and not take the risk of having an over-trained model on the data.

The algorithm used consists of evaluating one or several metrics each time a new tree is added to the set. If this or these metrics do not evolve during a fixed number n of iterations, only the trees having brought a gain are kept.

> ☞ It is important to note that the evaluation of the metrics at each iteration must be done at least on a test dataset, and not the training dataset, otherwise the error will reduce endlessly, as the model sticks to the training data.

The code listing below repeats the previous example, but activates early stopping, and sets the number of iterations n without additional gain to 20 :

```python
# ch3_early_stop.py
import numpy as np
from sklearn.datasets import make_classification
from sklearn.model_selection import train_test_split


from xgboost import XGBClassifier
import matplotlib.pyplot as plt

X, y = make_classification(n_samples=100,
                           n_informative=5,
                           n_classes=3,
                           random_state=5)

X_train, X_test, y_train, y_test = train_test_split(X,
    y, test_size=0.2, random_state=42)

eval_set = [(X_train, y_train), (X_test, y_test)]
model = XGBClassifier(use_label_encoder=False,
                      verbose=True,
                      num_class=3)

model.fit(X_train, y_train,
          early_stopping_rounds=10,
          eval_metric=['mlogloss'],
          eval_set=eval_set)
# [0] validation_0-mlogloss:0.80954
#     validation_1-mlogloss:0.91414
# [1] validation_0-mlogloss:0.61295
#     validation_1-mlogloss:0.80010
# [2] validation_0-mlogloss:0.46815
#     validation_1-mlogloss:0.72442
# [3] validation_0-mlogloss:0.36609
#     validation_1-mlogloss:0.66446
```

```
# [4] validation_0-mlogloss:0.29383
      validation_1-mlogloss:0.64616
# [5] validation_0-mlogloss:0.23800
      validation_1-mlogloss:0.61983
# [6] validation_0-mlogloss:0.19832
      validation_1-mlogloss:0.59875
# [7] validation_0-mlogloss:0.16526
      validation_1-mlogloss:0.58952
# [8] validation_0-mlogloss:0.14131
      validation_1-mlogloss:0.57995
# [9] validation_0-mlogloss:0.12145
      validation_1-mlogloss:0.57413
# [10] validation_0-mlogloss:0.10602
      validation_1-mlogloss:0.58198
print(model.best_iteration)
# -> 12
```

As stated in the code, the best score was obtained for a model with 12 trees.

The error evolution plot for the training and test datasets with this mechanism shows that overfitting was indeed avoided.

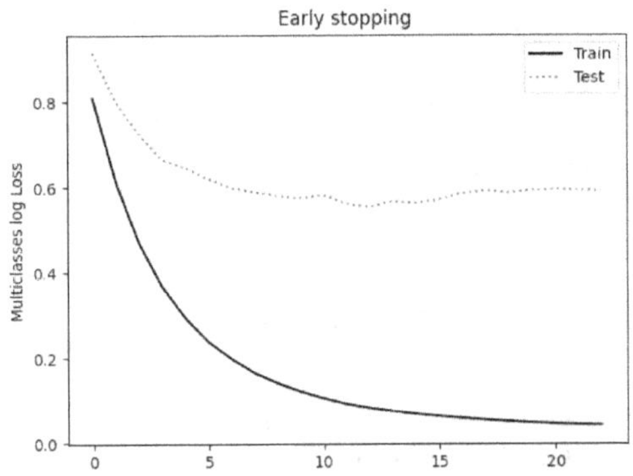


## 4.6  Application

### 4.6.1  Digits dataset

To illustrate the versatility of Gradient Boosting methods, the classification performed in this section will be done on images. The digits dataset, easily retrievable from the sklearn library contains 1797 handwritten digits, from 0 to 9.

To change from the previous examples, LightGBM, the third major implementation of Gradient Boosting, will be used. It has been developped by Microsoft.

### Default configuration

The images are first resized to make them vectors that LightGBM can handle. For this purpose, the reshape method is used.

The train_test_split method is invoked to automatically build a training dataset and a test dataset. The random_state has been set to 42, to ensure the reproducibility of the results.

> ☞ In general, when developing Machine Learning algorithms used in production, random states should not be fixed. Keeping the variability introduced by this recourse to chance is a guarantee of robustness.

The training is then started with the default configuration of the LGBMClassifier :

```python
# ch3_classification.py
from sklearn import datasets
import matplotlib.pyplot as plt
from lightgbm import LGBMClassifier
from sklearn.model_selection import train_test_split
from sklearn.metrics import accuracy_score,
    confusion_matrix

digits = datasets.load_digits()
images = digits.images
targets = digits.target

images=images.reshape(1797,8*8)

X_train, X_test, y_train, y_test = train_test_split(
    images, targets, test_size=0.3, random_state=42)

model = LGBMClassifier(objective='multiclass')
model.fit(X_train, y_train)
print(model.best_iteration_)

y_pred=model.predict(X_test)
accuracy = accuracy_score(y_test, y_pred)

print("Accuracy: %.2f%%" % (accuracy * 100.0))
# -> 97.78%
confusion = confusion_matrix(y_test, y_pred)
print('Matrix Confusion')
print(confusion)
# Confusion Matrix

# [[51 0 0 0 1 0 0 0 0 0]
# [ 1 51 0 0 0 0 0 0 0 0]
# [ 0 1 53 0 0 0 0 0 0 0]
```

```
# [ 0  0  0  56  0  0  0  1  0  0]
# [ 0  0  0  0  50  1  0  1  0  0]
# [ 0  0  0  0  0  0  50  0  0  2  0]
# [ 0  1  0  0  1  0  54  0  1  0]
# [ 0  0  0  0  0  0  0  62  0  0]
# [ 0  0  0  0  0  0  0  0  47  1]
# [ 0  0  0  1  0  1  0  0  0  52]]
```

The results obtained with this first simple version and without any particular optimization of the hyperparameters, nor concern for overfitting, are already very good.

The accuracy, which indicates that 97.78% of the test data was correctly classified, is quite high.

The confusion matrix confirms this result since it is diagonal. The most confused digit is the 9, which is taken once for a 3 and once for a 5.


**Simplification of the model**

The following listing adds early_stopping to try to counteract possible overfitting.

For this, a table containing the expected features and predictions was provided, both for the training dataset and the test dataset. Finally, a maximum of 10 iterations without progress was defined to activate the premature termination of the training:

```python
# ch3_classification_opt.py
from sklearn import datasets
import matplotlib.pyplot as plt
from lightgbm import LGBMClassifier
from sklearn.model_selection import train_test_split
from sklearn.metrics import accuracy_score,
    confusion_matrix

digits = datasets.load_digits()
images = digits.images
targets = digits.target

images=images.reshape(1797,8*8)

X_train, X_test, y_train, y_test = train_test_split(
                        images, targets,
                        test_size=0.3,
                        random_state=42)

eval_set = [(X_train, y_train), (X_test, y_test)]

model = LGBMClassifier(objective='multiclass',
                  n_estimators=500,
                  max_depth=10)
```

```python
model.fit(X_train, y_train,
          early_stopping_rounds=10,
          eval_metric=['logloss'],
          eval_set=eval_set)


print(model.best_iteration)
# -> 64
y_pred=model.predict(X_test,
                     start_iteratio=0,
                     num_iteration=model.best_iteration_)

accuracy = accuracy_score(y_test, y_pred)
print("Accuracy: %.2f%%" % (accuracy * 100.0))

confusion = confusion_matrix(y_test, y_pred)
print('Matrix Confusion')
print(confusion)
Accuracy: 97.78%.

Matrix Confusion

[[52  0  0  0  1  0  0  0  0  0]
 [ 0 49  1  0  0  0  0  0  0  0]
 [ 0  0 47  0  0  0  0  0  0  0]
 [ 0  0  1 53  0  0  0  0  0  0]
 [ 0  1  0  0 59  0  0  0  0  0]
 [ 0  0  0  0  1 64  1  0  0  0]
 [ 0  0  0  0  1  0 51  0  1  0]
 [ 0  0  0  0  0  0  0 55  0  0]
 [ 0  1  0  0  0  0  0  0 42  0]
 [ 1  0  0  0  0  0  0  1  1 56]]
```

The result is no better than with the previous configuration, but the complexity of the model has been reduced. Only 64 trees are now used, compared to 100 before. This is highlighted by the call to predict, for which the first and last tree to be applied have been specified.

This result can be further improved by using data enrichment, as presented at the very beginning of this chapter.

> ☞ Convolutional neural networks proceed in the same way, by enriching the initial images with automatically learned convolutions.

In the context of image processing, this enrichment is generally done using convolutions. In this field, it is classic to rely on edge detection filters such as the Sobel filter.

This is what the code below does, adding as a feature the result of applying a horizontal Sobel filter to the images:

```python
# ch3_classification_enrich.py
from sklearn import datasets
import numpy as np
import matplotlib.pyplot as plt
from lightgbm import LGBMClassifier
from sklearn.model_selection import train_test_split
from sklearn.metrics import accuracy_score,
    confusion_matrix
from sklearn.feature_extraction import image
from skimage import filters

digits = datasets.load_digits()
images = digits.images
targets = digits.target

patches_sobel_h = [filters.sobel_h(img).reshape(8*8)
    for img in images]

images = images.reshape(1797,8*8)
print(images.shape)

images = np.array([np.concatenate([img, patches_sobel_h
    [idx]]) for idx, img in enumerate(images)])
print(images.shape)

X_train, X_test, y_train, y_test = train_test_split(
                                images, targets,
                                test_size=0.3,
                                    random_state=42)
eval_set = [(X_train, y_train), (X_test, y_test)]

model = LGBMClassifier(objective='multiclass',
                    n_estimators=500,
                    max_depth=10)
model.fit(X_train, y_train,
        early_stopping_rounds=10,
        eval_metric=['logloss'],
        eval_set=eval_set
)


print(model.best_iteration_)
# -> 78
y_pred=model.predict(X_test,
                start_iteratio=0,
                num_iteration=model.best_iteration_)
accuracy = accuracy_score(y_test, y_pred)

print("Accuracy: %.2f%%" % (accuracy * 100.0))
# -> Accuracy:  98.15
```

```python
confusion = confusion_matrix(y_test, y_pred)
print('Matrix Confusion')
print(confusion)
# [[53  0  0  0  0  0  0  0  0  0]
#  [ 0 49  1  0  0  0  0  0  0  0]
#  [ 0  0 47  0  0  0  0  0  0  0]
#  [ 0  0  2 51  0  0  0  0  1  0]
#  [ 0  1  0  0 59  0  0  0  0  0]
#  [ 0  0  0  1  1 64  0  0  0  0]
#  [ 0  0  0  0  1  0 52  0  0  0]
#  [ 0  0  0  0  0  0  0 55  0  0]
#  [ 0  0  0  0  0  0  0  0 43  0]
#  [ 0  0  0  1  0  0  0  0  1 57]]
```

The accuracy increases by more than 0.3%, to exceed 98%, which is quite honorable. This illustrates well the gains brought by data enrichment, which is in this case endogenous since it is obtained from the data itself. The confusion matrix confirms this result, as the number 1 for example is no longer confused with 4.

# Chapter 5

# Understanding and explaining a model

## 5.1 Explicability

### 5.1.1 Motivation

Decision trees, when trained using the Gradient Boosting method, can achieve very high levels of performance.

On tabular data, in particular, they have nothing to envy to Deep Learning based approaches. They regularly come out on top in many data science competitions and are widely deployed in Machine Learning applications. They have the clear advantage over neural approaches of a shorter training time and greater ease of configuration.

This level of performance does not come without a downside, which they share with Deep Learning methods: they suffer from the black box effect. It is difficult, as soon as the generated models contain several trees, to understand the impact of the input features on the generated predictions.

Understanding the importance, weight, and direction of the effect of each input feature on output prediction is crucial for at least three reasons.

First, this understanding is a valuable guide for the data scientist. It informs him about the relevance of his model and points out areas for improvement.

Secondly, it ensures credibility to the generated model with the end user, reassures them of its relevance, and facilitates its adoption. It is also a powerful means of appropriation of the model by the craftsman, who will find his expertise through this transparency.

Finally, in the case where the purpose of the model is to understand a phenomenon, this analysis phase is essential. It will allow logic to emerge from a set of complex data that would have escaped the human eye due to the volume and/or the high dimensionality of the data.

This capacity to account for the predictions made by a model is called explicability. It can be studied at two levels: global and local.

## 5.1.2   Global view

At the global level, the goal of explicability is to account for the criteria used to construct the decision trees.

This provides a global view of the model and gives macro information on the data or features that have been used.

The data scientist can then use these explanations to ensure that his model uses all the information available to him and has not unduly excluded useful data.

On the other hand, in the case where the purpose of the model is to understand a phenomenon, after having been able to predict it, the insights provided by explainability are valuable.

## 5.1.3   Local view

In a local analysis, the objective is to understand in detail what motivated a particular prediction.

It is no longer a question of having a high-level view of the model, but of being able to explain in detail why such a class or such a value has been predicted.

This level of explicability is particularly important to convince and engage the user of the Machine Learning application by showing him precisely how the machine comes to this result.

## 5.1.4   Particularity of decision trees

The best way to explain a model is usually in the model itself. After all, the purpose of modeling is to pose formulas and establish relationships between input information and the target to be predicted.

This is done, for example, by the equations of Newtonian mechanics, which account for the motion of solid bodies subjected to forces. The analysis of these equations establishes the proportionality between force and acceleration, then the differential relation between acceleration and velocity, and finally between velocity and position.

Explainability is an inherent part of the model.

Unfortunately, not all systems are as simple as solid body mechanics, and as soon as the relationships between inputs and outputs become non-linear, it becomes difficult to put a simple model on them.

The strength of models based on decision trees is that they can tackle these problems which are difficult to model otherwise. This plasticity is paid for by an apparent complexity, linked to the superposition of numerous trees.

Simply reading the generated trees is not enough. More sophisticated methods must be used to make them intelligible.

The following two sections detail them.

## 5.2 Feature importances

### 5.2.1 Presentation

The method used commonly for the three main implementations XGBoost, CatBoost, and LightGBM is the feature importance. It assigns to each feature a weight giving an idea of its global importance.

It is therefore not a method that allows a local view, at the resolution of the prediction.

Several ways of calculating these weights are possible, depending on whether the focus is on gain, weights, or other indicators such as coverage.

### 5.2.2 Calculation based on the level of use

According to this calculation mode, the weight is given for each feature by the number of times it is involved in a decision node, to separate the data into two subsets. This mode is called weight mode.

This gives an idea of how much the feature is used to ensure a good level of prediction. This usually implies an extended value range for the feature, since the Gradient Boosting method has found it relevant to break it into many different value ranges.

This dependency on the cardinality of the feature can introduce a bias in the explainability, as a feature with a large cardinality is likely to be used in many nodes.

### 5.2.3 Calculation based on gain

In this calculation mode, named gain, the weight is calculated by averaging the gains obtained when the considered feature was used as a criterion of splitting of the data set.

This gives each feature an average idea of the impact of this feature on the reduction of the error. The advantage of this calculation is that it gives a precise idea of the contribution of the feature in terms of gain to the model, independently of the number of times it is used.

### 5.2.4   Calculation based on coverage

The last class of feature importance calculation mode is based on the coverage, i.e. the number of samples concerned by the decision taken for the feature considered. It is called cover.

In this case, the importance gives an idea of the volume of observations that have been impacted by this feature, and thus an idea of the impact of this feature on the predictions.

Two calculation modes are possible: either the number of associated samples is averaged, or it is summed.

### 5.2.5   Implementation

To fully understand the different ways of calculating the feature importance, the code presented in the chapter on the operation of the Gradient Boosting method has been augmented to include them.

It includes the DecisionNode class, which allows to create a node, to evaluate the condition attached to it, and to navigate from node to node.

```python
# ch4_feature_importance.py
import matplotlib.pyplot as plt
import pandas as pd
from jax import grad, jacfwd, jacrev, jit
import jax.numpy as jnp
import numpy as np
from sklearn.datasets import load_boston
from sklearn.model_selection import train_test_split
import matplotlib.pyplot as plt

import random, pickle

class DecisionNode:
    def __init__(self, name, condition,
                 value=None, depth=0,
                 label=None):
        self.name = name
        self.condition = condition
        self.label = label
        self.value = value
```

```python
        self.left = None
        self.right = None
        self.depth = depth

    def add_left_node(self, left):
        self.left = left

    def add_right_node(self, right):
        self.right = right

    def is_leaf(self):
        return (not self.left) and (not self.right)

    def next(self, data):
        cond = self.condition(data)
        if cond:
            return self.left
        else:
        return self.right
```

The DecisionEnsemble class has been modified, in particular,
to add a feature_importances dictionary which will contain the information useful to calculate the three different types of feature
importances: weights, gains, and cover.

```python
class DecisionEnsemble:
    def __init__(self, nb_estimators, max_depth,
                 gamma=0, lbda=0):
        self.roots = [DecisionNode(f'root_{esti}', None
            , 0.0) for esti in range(0, nb_estimators)]
        self.lbda = lbda
        self.gamma = gamma
        self.objective = lambda y_pred, y_true: np.dot(
            y_true - y_pred, (y_true - y_pred).T)
        self.grad = lambda y_pred, y_true: -2 * (y_true
            - y_pred)
        self.hessian = lambda y_pred, y_true: np.array
            ([2] * y_pred.shape[0])
        self.max_depth = max_depth
        self.base_score = None
        self.feature_importances = {'weights': {},
                                    'earnings': {},
                                    cover: {}}


    def _create_condition(self, col_name, split_value):
        return lambda dta : dta[col_name] < split_value

    def _add_child_nodes(self, node, nodes,
                         node_x, node_y,
                         split_value, split_column,
```

```python
                    nb_nodes,
                    left_w, right_w, prev_w):
    node.condition = self._create_condition(
        split_column, split_value) # we must create
        a closure to capture split_value copy
    node.label = f'{split_column} < {split_value}'
    node.add_left_node(DecisionNode(f'left_{
        nb_nodes}',

                            None, left_w +
                                prev_w,
                            depth = node.depth
                                +1))
    node.add_right_node(DecisionNode(f'right_{
        nb_nodes}',

                            None, right_w +
                                prev_w,
                            depth = node.depth
                                +1))
    mask = node_x[split_column] < split_value
    # Reverse order to ensure bfs
    nodes.append((node.left,
            node_x[mask].copy(),
            node_y[mask].copy(),
            left_w + prev_w))
    nodes.append((node.right,
            node_x[~mask].copy(),
            node_y[~mask].copy(),
            right_w + prev_w))
```

> ☞ For performance and code simplification reasons, the
> DecisionEnsemble class has been modified to no longer
> take the objective function as an argument. It has been
> hard-coded with the squared error. This limits its use
> to the case of regression.

The fit method, which does the actual learning, concentrates
the core of the modifications. In particular, it is important to
note that unlike the code in the chapter illustrating how Gradient
Boosting works, the column used to partition the data at a node
is no longer taken at random.

On the contrary, all columns are evaluated, and the one with
the most significant gain is finally kept. Without this completeness,
the calculated metrics would not be correct, especially in the case
of the weights calculation mode.

```python
def fit(self, x_train, y_train):
    self.base_score = y_train.mean()
    self.roots[0].value = self.base_score
    node_count = 0
```

```python
for tree_idx, tree_root in enumerate(self.roots
    ):
    # store current node (currently a lead),
        x_train, and node leaf weight
    nodes = [(tree_root, x_train.copy(), y_train
        .copy(), 0.0)]
    nb_nodes = 0
    real_depth = 0
    # Add node to tree using bfs
    while nodes:
        node, node_x, node_y, prev_w = nodes.pop
            (0)
        node_x['pred'] = self.predict(node_x)
        best_gain = None
        cols = x_train.columns.tolist()
        for split_column in cols:
            split, split_value, left_w, \
                right_w, left_gain, right_gain, \
                gain = self._find_best_split(
                    split_column,
                    node_x, node_y,
                    nb_nodes)
            if best_gain is None:
                best_gain = gain
            if gain >= best_gain:
                best_split_column = split_column
                best_split = split
                best_split_value = split_value
                best_left_w = left_w
                best_right_w = right_w
                best_prev_w = prev_w
                best_left_gain = left_gain
                best_right_gain = right_gain
        if best_split != -1 and node.depth <
            self.max_depth:
            self._add_child_nodes(node, nodes,
                                node_x, node_y,
                                best_split_value,

                                best_split_column
                                ,
                                node_count,
                                best_left_w,
                                    best_right_w,
                                    best_prev_w)
            self._update_feature_importances(
                best_split_column,

                                best_left_gain
                                +
                                best_right_gai
                                ,
```

```
                                                    node_x.
                                                      shape
                                                      [0])

            node_count += 2
            real_depth += 1
        nb_nodes += 1
        if nb_nodes >= 2**self.max_depth-1:
        break
```

Once the feature bringing maximum gain is identified, a call is
made to the _update_feature_importances method, which will store
the information useful to the three calculation modes, namely: the
gain which is the sum of the left and right gains, the cover, which
is the number of observations concerned by the partition for the
considered node, and finally the weight which is the number of
times the feature is used in a node.

```
def _update_feature_importances(self, feature_name,
    gain, cover):
    self.feature_importances['gains'][feature_name]
        = self.feature_importances['gains'].get(
    feature_name, []) + [float(gain)]
    self.feature_importances['cover'][feature_name]
        = self.feature_importances['cover'].get(
    feature_name, []) + [float(cover)]
    self.feature_importances['weights'][
        feature_name] = self.feature_importances['
    weights'].get(feature_name, 0) + 1
The rest of the code takes care of the calculation of
    the gains and the search for the best partitioning
    criterion, according to the formulas given in the
    chapter on the operation of Gradient Boosting :
def _gain_and_weight(self, x_train, y_train,
    nb_nodes):
    pred = x_train['pred'].values
    G_i = self.grad(pred, y_train.values).sum()
    H_i = self.hessian(pred, y_train.values).sum()
    return -0.5 * G_i * G_i / (H_i + self.lbda) +
        self.gamma * nb_nodes, -G_i / (H_i + self.
        lbda)

def _find_best_split(self, col_name, node_x, node_y
    , nb_nodes):
    x_sorted = node_x.sort_values(by=col_name)
    y_sorted = node_y[x_sorted.index]
    current_gain, _ = self._gain_and_weight(
        x_sorted, node_y, nb_nodes)
    gain = 0.0
    best_split = -1
    split_value, best_left_w, best_right_w,
```

```python
            best_left_gain, best_right_gain = None, None
            , None, None, None
        for split_idx in range(1, x_sorted.shape[0]):
            # skip equal value
            if split_idx <x_sorted.shape[0]-1:
                if x_sorted.iloc[split_idx][col_name] ==
                    x_sorted.iloc[split_idx+1][col_name
                    ]:
                    continues
            left_data = x_sorted.iloc[:split_idx]
            right_data = x_sorted.iloc[split_idx:]
            left_y = y_sorted.iloc[:split_idx]
            right_y = y_sorted.iloc[split_idx:]
            left_gain, left_w = self._gain_and_weight(
                left_data, left_y, nb_nodes)
            right_gain, right_w = self._gain_and_weight(
                right_data, right_y, nb_nodes)
            if current_gain - (left_gain + right_gain) >
                gain:
                gain = current_gain - (left_gain +
                    right_gain)
                best_split = split_idx
                split_value = x_sorted[col_name].iloc[
                    split_idx]
                best_left_w = left_w
                best_right_w = right_w
                best_left_gain = left_gain
                best_right_gain = right_gain
        return best_split, split_value, best_left_w,
            best_right_w, best_left_gain,
            best_right_gain, gain

    def predict(self, data):
        preds = []
        for _, row in data.iterrows():
            pred = 0.0
            for tree_idx, root in enumerate(self.roots):
                child = root
                while child and not child.is_leaf():
                    child = child.next(row)
                pred += child.value
            preds.append(pred)
        return np.array(preds) + self.base_score
```

The implementation of the calculation of the importance of each
feature, according to a global view, is thus done immediately, and
with a negligible additional cost both in terms of calculation time
and storage.

This is why it is implemented by default by the three main
Gradient Boosting libraries for decision trees: XGBoost, CatBoost,

and LightGBM.

The didactic implementation presented above is used transparently, as shown in the following example based on the Boston dataset:

```python
boston = load_boston()

x_train, x_test, y_train, y_test = train_test_split(
    boston.data, boston.target, test_size=0.2,
    random_state=42)

y_train = pd.DataFrame({"Y" : y_train})
x_train = pd.DataFrame(x_train, columns=boston.
    feature_names)
x_test = pd.DataFrame(x_test, columns=boston.
    feature_names)
tree = DecisionEnsemble(squared_error, 50, 3)

tree.fit(x_train, y_train['Y'])
pred = tree.predict(x_test)
print(pred)
#-> [21.7, 28.47, 21.7 28.47, 13.06, 28.47, ...

mean = {k: abs(np.mean(v)) for k,v in tree.
    feature_importances['gains'].items()}
print(mean)
# ->  'LSTAT': -6905.327611957848, 'CRIM':
    -155.85076530601873, 'PTRATIO': -39.75703359393743,
    'TAX': -117.44408069160463, 'DIS':
    -162.58054656898864, 'RM': -466.72327934543711, 'B':
    -104.72029666312362, 'RAD': -117.37806885091399,
    'AGE': -41.44753960487419, 'NOX':
    -58.25049793614738, 'INDUS': -83.88902121942156,
    'ZN': -43.02020051516297, 'CHAS':
    -11.362683360304638
```

Here, the average gain for each feature is calculated. Classically this information is represented in the form of a bar chart:

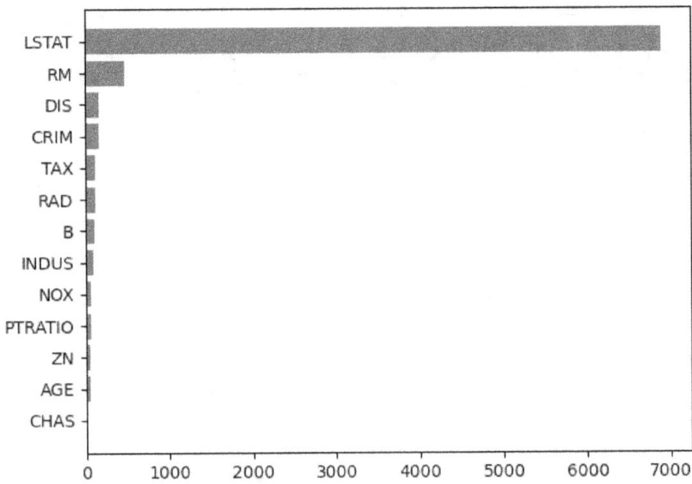

This shows that the bulk of the information is carried by the LSTAT column, followed far behind by RM, then CRIM. The following lines of code achieve much the same result using XGBoost :

```python
# ch4_feature_importance_xgb.py
from sklearn.datasets import load_boston
from sklearn.model_selection import train_test_split
import matplotlib.pyplot as plt
from xgboost import XGBRegressor

boston = load_boston()

x_train, x_test, y_train, y_test = train_test_split(
    boston.data, boston.target, test_size=0.2,
    random_state=42)

print({ boston.feature_names[idx]: importance for idx,
    importance in enumerate(xgb.feature_importances_)})
# ->  'CRIM': 0.022315497, 'ZN': 0.0013826311, 'INDUS':
    0.00687292, 'CHAS': 0.0027196791, 'NOX':
    0.050526466, 'RM': 0.35646823, 'AGE': 0.015537402,
    'DIS': 0.039626102, 'RAD': 0.00882377, 'TAX':
    0.034043133, 'PTRATIO': 0.03112754, 'B':
    0.009297607, 'LSTAT': 0.42125916
```

The gains have been normalized and are therefore not the same as with the simplified implementation above. However, the order of importance is essentially the same, as shown in the graph below:

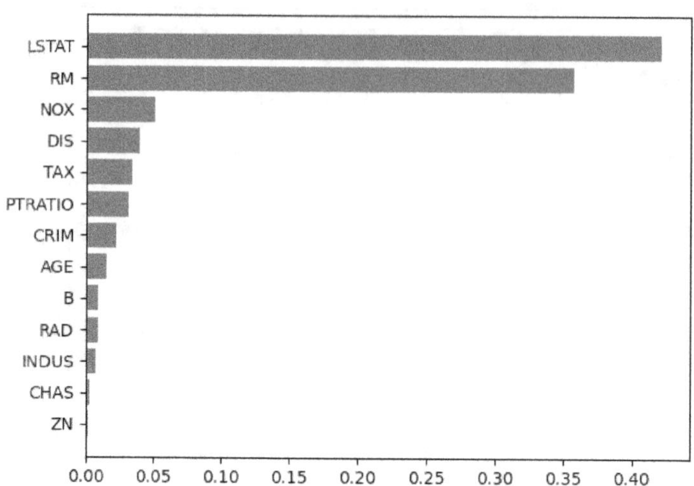

## 5.2.6   Interpretation of the three calculation modes

It is important to understand how to interpret the values associated
with these three calculation modes. To do this, the following code
calculates, using XGBoost, these metrics for each mode:

```python
# ch4_feature_importance_xgb.py
from sklearn.datasets import load_boston
from sklearn.model_selection import train_test_split
import matplotlib.pyplot as plt
from xgboost import XGBRegressor

boston = load_boston()

x_train, x_test, y_train, y_test = train_test_split(
    boston.data, boston.target, test_size=0.2,
    random_state=42)

xgb = XGBRegressor(n_estimators=50, importance_type="
    cover")
xgb.fit(x_train, y_train)
sorted_idx = xgb.feature_importances_.argsort()
print({boston.feature_names[idx]:xgb.
    feature_importances_[idx] for idx in sorted_idx})
# ->   'ZN': 0.027104674, 'INDUS': 0.036392692, 'CRIM':
    0.03985535, 'RAD': 0.060898088, 'CHAS': 0.06657668,
    'NOX': 0.0733411, 'RM': 0.08605623, 'PTRATIO':
    0.08794409, 'B': 0.09772734, 'DIS': 0.0979996,
```

```python
'AGE': 0.101690546, 'LSTAT': 0.11076217, 'TAX':
0.11365144

xgb = XGBRegressor(n_estimators=50, importance_type="
    gain")
xgb.fit(x_train, y_train)
sorted_idx = xgb.feature_importances_.argsort()
print({boston.feature_names[idx]:xgb.
    feature_importances_[idx] for idx in sorted_idx})
# ->  'ZN': 0.0013826311, 'CHAS': 0.0027196791,
    'INDUS': 0.00687292, 'RAD': 0.00882377, 'B':
    0.009297607, 'AGE': 0.015537402, 'CRIM':
    0.022315497, 'PTRATIO': 0.03112754, 'TAX':
    0.034043133, 'DIS': 0.03962602, 'NOX': 0.050526466,
    'RM': 0.35646823, 'LSTAT': 0.42125916

xgb = XGBRegressor(n_estimators=50, importance_type="
    weight")
xgb.fit(x_train, y_train)
sorted_idx = xgb.feature_importances_.argsort()
print({boston.feature_names[idx]:xgb.
    feature_importances_[idx] for idx in sorted_idx})
# ->  'CHAS': 0.008130081, 'RAD': 0.011517615, 'ZN':
    0.021680217, 'INDUS': 0.034552846, 'PTRATIO':
    0.034552846, 'TAX': 0.03726287, 'NOX': 0.061653115,
    'B': 0.09485095, 'LSTAT': 0.0995935, 'AGE':
    0.10704607, 'DIS': 0.10704607, 'RM': 0.16192412,
    'CRIM': 0.2201897
```

The one that provides the most information on the contribution of a feature in terms of model performance is the gain mode. Indeed, the gain corresponds to the contribution of the feature to the reduction of the model error.

The features that are ranked the highest with this method of calculation are the features that contribute the most to the improvement of the model's performance. The diagram below lists them by decreasing gain:

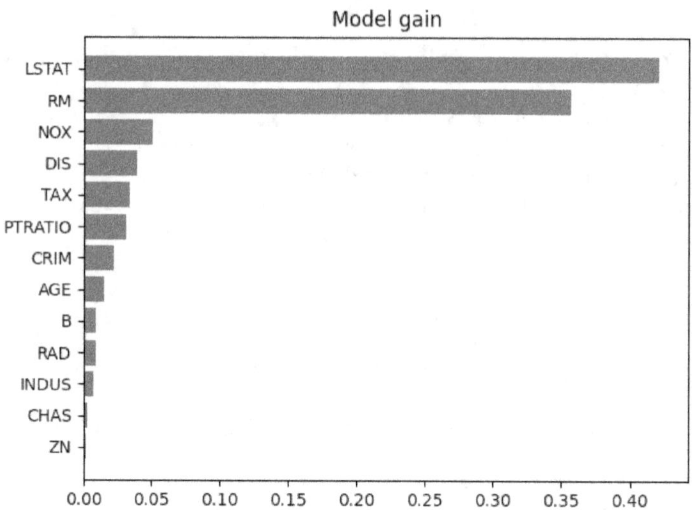

The second mode that is interesting to analyze is the cover mode, which provides information on the volume of training data that has passed through the filter of the feature considered.

In the example used here, the following graph is obtained:

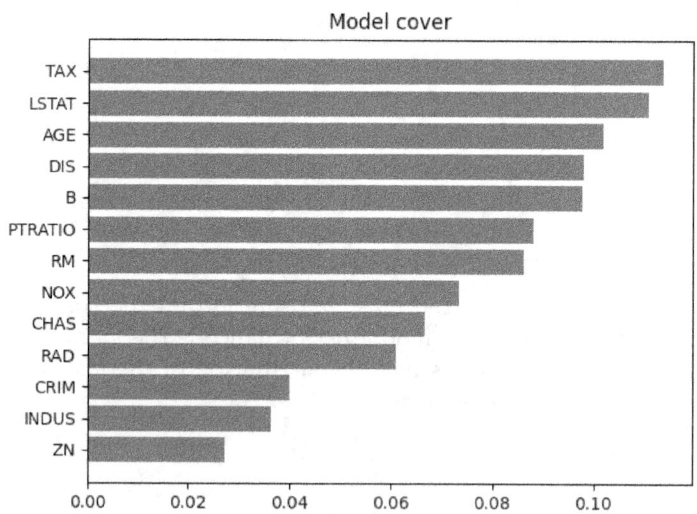

It is interesting to note that the feature that brought a significant gain, CRIM, does so based on a few observations. This highlights the fact that there is a different and marked behavior for a subset of the data. The model identified this group and made a relevant correction.

The opposite phenomenon occurs for the LSTAT feature, which has a large cover and a relatively high gain. This means that the impact of this feature is generalized and does not concern particular subsets.

## 5.3   SHAP: SHapley Additive exPlanation

The previous section presented the feature importance, which shed quantitative light on the role of each feature both in the construction of the model and in the prediction. Their explanatory value is nevertheless limited to a global view.

In this section, the SHAP method, Shapley Additive exPlanation, will be presented. It offers a finer understanding of a model, by allowing it to go down to the prediction level. It is a recent method, which was first published in 2016.

It also provides a more detailed view, by detailing the impact of each feature in a quantitative and signed way. This means that it informs about the direction in which the prediction has been made: upwards or downwards. This is a very important insight into how the model works.

Finally, it is a generic method that can be applied to any type of model, from deep neural networks to SVMs, including of course decision trees.

### 5.3.1   Objective: build an explanatory model

In the case where a linear model is used to make a prediction, the prediction is calculated with the following formula:

$$p_k = \alpha_0 + \alpha_1 x_1 + \alpha_2 x_2 + \alpha_3 x_3 + \ldots$$

The prediction is then a linear combination of each feature $x_i$. The weight of a feature i in the prediction k is then the product of the ith coefficient alpha with the value of the ith feature.

Such a model directly embeds an additive explanatory model, since the prediction is the sum of each weight multiplied by each feature. If the coefficient is positive, then the feature influences the prediction upwards. If it is negative, the prediction is pulled down. The absolute value of the product of the feature and the coefficient gives the importance of this feature in the sense of Shapley.

The objective of the SHAP method is to propose a procedure to automatically build such a model, which is locally additive. In a way, it is a matter of linearizing the predictive model, as complex as it is, to extract a linear explanatory model. In mathematical form, this explanatory model g is expressed as follows:

$$g_x(z') = \phi_0 + \sum_{j=1}^{M} \phi_j z_j'$$

Where the vector z' contains only 0's and 1's. The presence of a 1 in $z_j$ indicates that the feature $x_j$ is used, while a 0 indicates that it is not.

M is the dimension of the vector z, which in the general case is the same as vector x dimension.

Applying this principle to the linear model calculating $p_k$ given above, it can be reformulated as follows:

$$p_{k,x} = \alpha_0 + (\alpha_1 x_1)z_1' + (\alpha_2 x_2)z_2' + (\alpha_3 x_3)z_3' + \ldots$$

This reformulation immediately highlights the fact that in the case of a linear model, for a given prediction, the associated Shapley values are obtained by multiplying the coefficients by their associated features.

The local aspect of the model is reflected in the notation using the index x attached to g. This implies that the explanatory model created is only valid for a fixed feature vector x. This also explains why the values of the elements $x_i$ of x can be substituted by the 0 and 1 of the vector z since the knowledge of the values of x is encoded in the model.

### 5.3.2 Shapley values

The type of model described above is additive by construction, but there are infinite possibilities for decomposing a number into a sum of n numbers.

Fortunately, by requiring the following properties for feature importance values:

- Local accuracy: the sum of the feature importances must be equal to the prediction.

- Absence: if a feature does not participate in the model, then the associated importance must be null.

- Consistency: if two models are compared, and the contribution of one model to a feature is greater than the other, then the feature importance must also be greater than the other model

There is only one possibility left: the Shapley values. Several formulas exist to compute them, depending on how the possibilities of sub-models are counted. The easiest one to implement is:

$$\phi_i = \frac{1}{n!} \sum_R \left[ f(P_i^R \cup i) - f(P_i^R) \right]$$

Where n specifies the number of features present in the model, R is the set of possible permutations for these features, $P_i^R$ is the list of features with an index lower than i of the considered permutation, and f is the model whose Shapley values must be computed.

> ☞ The number of permutations of a set of dimension n is the factorial of n, hence the n ! in factor of the sum

The working principle of this method is simple and generic. It applies to any type of model: it consists in building a model without the feature i for each possible sub-model. For this, all possible permutations are scanned. The difference between the prediction obtained for each model and the same model with the considered feature is then calculated. The average of this difference gives the feature importance according to Shapley.

Although very simple, this formula is very intensive in terms of computation time in the general case, as the number of models to be trained increases factorially with the number of features.

With two features $x_1$, $x_2$, 2 models can be built for feature 1: 1 without any feature, 1 with only $x_2$.

With three features, it is already more complex. 6 models can be built: 2 without feature, 1 with $x_2$ , 1 with $x_3$ , 1 with $x_2$ and $x_3$, and 1 with $x_3$ and $x_2$.

The operation must be repeated for each prediction.

### 5.3.3  Implementation

**Linear model**

To understand this concept, an implementation of the SHAP method is given below, first for linear models:

```python
# ch4_linear_SHAP.py
from itertools import permutations
import math

import numpy as np
from sklearn.datasets import make_regression
from sklearn.linear_model import LinearRegression
```

```python
from matplotlib import pyplot as plt


def list_all_possible_perumations(nb_features):
    features = set(range(0, nb_features))
    return [cmb for cmb in permutations(features)]
```
This first function lists all possible permutations for
n features. It thus constructs the set R of the
previous formula.

```python
def compute_theta_i(model, nb_features, data,
    feature_excluded):
    ordering = list_all_possible_perumations(
        nb_features, feature_excluded)
    theta = 0.0
    for subset in ordering:
        subset = list(subset)
        feature_idx = subset.index(feature_excluded)
        data_without_feature = [[x if subset.index(i) <
            feature_idx else 0 for i, x in enumerate(
            data)]]
        data_with_feature = [[x if subset.index(i) <=
            feature_idx else 0 for i, x in enumerate(
            data)]]
        weight = 1.0 / len(ordering)
        theta += weight * (model.predict(
            data_with_feature)[0] - model.predict(
            data_without_feature)[0])
    return theta
```

This compute_theta_i function forms the core of the method
since it will compute the theta value for a given feature i. To do
this, it goes through all possible permutations, builds the sets with
and without the feature, and finally uses the model to make the
two predictions, the difference of which is computed.

The sum of these differences is then calculated, weighted by the
inverse of the factorial of the number of features.

The code is then tested on two models trained on regression
data using this function:

```python
def train_linear_model(n_features):
    x_train, y_train = make_regression(n_samples=100,
                                       n_features=
                                           n_features,
                                       n_informative=
                                           n_features,
                                       noise=1,
                                       random_state=42)

    model = LinearRegression(fit_intercept=True)
    model.fit(x_train, y_train)
```

```
    return x_train, y_train, model
```

The first model uses only two features. The theta values obtained are consistent with the theory since they are equal to the product of the feature and the corresponding coefficient of the regression:

```
n_features = 2
x_train, y_train, model = train_linear_model(n_features
    )
theta = []
for feature_idx in range(0,n_features):
    theta.append(compute_theta_i(model, n_features,
        list(x_train[0]), feature_idx))
print(theta[0], model.coef_[0] * x_train[0][0])
# -> -104.31510227037786 -104.31510227037786
print(theta[1], model.coef_[1] * x_train[0][1])
# -> 48.63805006076018 48.63805006076018
print(np.sum(theta) + model.intercept_, model.predict(
    x_train[[0]])[0])
# -> -55.655416401171586 -55.655416401171586
The same is true for a model with 3 features:
n_features = 3
x_train, y_train, model = train_linear_model(n_features
    )
theta = []
for feature_idx in range(0,n_features):
    theta.append(compute_theta_i(model, n_features,
        list(x_train[0]), feature_idx))
print(theta[0], model.coef_[0] * x_train[0][0])
# -> -22.36084079197455 -22.36084079197455
print(theta[1], model.coef_[1] * x_train[0][1])
# -> 37.85105905959119 37.85105905959119
print(theta[2], model.coef_[2] * x_train[0][2])
# -> -2.0479756083176737 -2.0479756083176737
print(np.sum(theta) + model.intercept_, model.predict(
    x_train[[0]])[0])
# -> 13.567167816890098 13.567167816890098
```

This confirms that the implementation is correct and provides the results predicted by the theory.

### Generic model

To support any type of model, you just need to modify the previous code to perform a re-training for each subset of features.

> ☞ In the case of a linear model, it is not useful to retrain. Indeed, a linear model is by nature additive, and removing a feature is the same as not taking it into account, by assigning it a null value

The updated code follows:

```python
# ch4_generic_SHAP.py
from itertools import permutations
import math

import numpy as np
import xgboost as xgb
import shap
from sklearn.datasets import make_regression
from sklearn.linear_model import LinearRegression
from matplotlib import pyplot as plt


def list_all_possible_perumations(nb_features):
    features = set(range(0, nb_features))
    return [cmb for cmb in permutations(features)]
```

The calculation of the different permutations remained the same. A ZeroModel class has been introduced to allow training models without any features. By convention, this type of model returns zero:

```python
class ZeroModel():
    def predict(self, dummy):
        return [0.0]
```

The function performing the training has been changed to take the useful data. This time it no longer trains a linear model, but an XGBoost model for regression.

The number of estimators and the depth were reduced to avoid overfitting.

Indeed, in the case of overfitting, the computed Shapley values are not valid, because the model has enough freedom to fit the data, even with a single feature. It then makes an almost exact prediction in each case, and all features end up with the same Shapley value.

```python
def train_model(x_train, y_train):
    # model with an empty feature set returns 0 by
        construction
    if x_train.shape[1] == 0:
        return ZeroModel()

    model = xgb.XGBRegressor(n_estimators=5,
                             max_depth=3)
    model.fit(x_train, y_train)
    return model
```

And finally, the method computing the Shapley values themselves has been modified to perform the re-training. The most interesting part concerns the generation of feature sets with and without the feature to be weighted:

```python
def compute_theta_i(x_train, y_train,
                    data,
                    feature_excluded):
    nb_features =x_train.shape[1]
    ordering = list_all_possible_perumations(
        nb_features)
    theta = 0.0
    for subset in ordering:
        subset = list(subset)
        feature_idx = subset.index(feature_excluded)

        subset_with_feature = sorted([fidx for _, fidx
            in enumerate(subset) if subset.index(fidx)
            <= feature_idx])
        subset_without_feature = sorted([fidx for _,
            fidx in enumerate(subset) if subset.index(
            fidx) < feature_idx])

        weight = 1.0 / len(ordering)
        model_with_feature = train_model(x_train[:,
            subset_with_feature], y_train)
        model_without_feature = train_model(x_train[:,
            subset_without_feature], y_train)

        data_with_feature = np.array([[x for i, x in
            enumerate(data) if i in subset_with_feature
            ]])
        data_without_feature = np.array([[x for i, x in
            enumerate(data) if i in
            subset_without_feature]])

        theta += weight * (model_with_feature.predict(
            data_with_feature)[0] - \
                        model_without_feature.predict(
                            data_without_feature)[0])
    return theta
```

This new implementation can then be tested on the same datasets as before. The shap library is also used to ensure that the computed values are consistent.

```python
n_features = 2
x_train, y_train = make_regression(n_samples=100,
                                   n_features=n_features,
                                   n_informative=
                                       n_features,
                                   noise=1,
                                   random_state=42)

theta = []
model_full = train_model(x_train, y_train)
explainer = shap.Explainer(model_full)
```

```python
shap_values = explainer(x_train)

for feature_idx in range(0,n_features):
    theta.append(compute_theta_i(x_train, y_train,
                            list(x_train[0]),
                            feature_idx))
    print(f'fi_{feature_idx}', theta[feature_idx],
        shap_values[0].values[feature_idx])
# -> fi_0 -68.42814254760742 -82.14687
# -> fi_1 21.016868591308594 41.031513

print(np.sum(theta) + (model_full.base_score or 0),
    model_full.predict(x_train[[0]])[0])
# -> -47.41127395629883 -47.411274
```

The local accuracy property is well respected since the sum of
the Shapley values gives the predicted value.

Moreover, the values obtained by this code are identical in terms
of sign with those provided by the shap library. The orders of
magnitude are comparable.

With more complex data, the gap narrows further:

```python
n_features = 3
x_train, y_train = make_regression(n_samples=100,
                            n_features=n_features,
                            n_informative=
                                n_features,
                            noise=1,
                            random_state=42)

theta = []
model_full = train_model(x_train, y_train)
explainer = shap.Explainer(model_full)
shap_values = explainer(x_train)
for feature_idx in range(0,n_features):
    theta.append(compute_theta_i(x_train, y_train,
                            list(x_train[0]),
                            feature_idx))
    print(f'fi_{feature_idx}', theta[feature_idx],
        shap_values[0].values[feature_idx])
# -> fi_0 -5.386728286743163 -5.900916
# -> fi_1 11.116163094838459 11.959647
# -> fi_2 2.7234941323598223 -1.0982516

print(np.sum(theta) + (model_full.base_score or 0),
    model_full.predict(x_train[[0]])[0])
# -> 8.452928940455118 8.452929
```

This discrepancy is due to the method used by the shap library,
which takes advantage of the structure of the decision trees to not
recalculate all the models as it has been done here.

## 5.3.4  Shapley value for decision trees

The method in the previous subsection was presented for pedagogical purposes only. In reality, the need to build n factorial models is prohibitive. For even 5 features, one has to train no less than 5!=120 models, and this as many times as there are predictions to analyze.

Fortunately, there is a solution, proposed by the authors of the SHAP method, to take advantage of the structure of decision trees and drastically reduce the computation time. It is then only necessary to train one model.

> ☞ The generic method of computing Shapley values is an NP-complete problem. That is, there is no method to compute them in polynomial time.

### Stored information for decision trees

As reminded in the second section of this chapter, when constructing decision trees, the gain, weight, and cover are stored for each node. These values are used to compute the feature importance but can be used to compute a good estimate of the Shapley values at a low cost.

### Evaluation for the SHAP method

In a companion paper to their first publication on the subject, Lundberg and Lee presented a polynomial-time implementation for computing Shapley values in the case of decision trees.

The idea is to use a single model, and thus avoid having to train a rapidly exponential number of models. To do this, they use the weights associated with the leaves and the cover. The goal is to obtain, from this single model, predictions for all possible combinations of features.

The method is as follows: for a given observation, and for the feature for which the Shapley value is to be calculated, it is sufficient to browse the decision trees of the model.

At each node, if the decision involves one of the features of the subset, everything happens as a standard path. If on the other hand the decision of the node is made from a feature that has not been retained by the subset, it is not possible to choose which branch of the tree to follow. In this case, both branches are explored, and the resulting weights are weighted by the cover, i.e. by the number of observations concerned by the test.

All that remains is to calculate the difference between the sub-model without the feature and the sub-model with the feature and to average it out.

This strategy is used in the SHAP library that was used above to validate the generic implementation presented.

### 5.3.5  Interpretation and visualization of Shapley values

The best way to interpret the Shapley values for a given prediction is to keep in mind the underlying mathematical formulation: it is a local additive linear model of the prediction.

The values are therefore only valid in the vicinity of the values of a given observation.

**Local explainability**

There are several ways to represent Shapley values, usually in the form of a bar chart as was done for the classical importance feature in the second section. Only this time, the data is signed.

Other representations are possible. The following few lines show the waterfall graph provided by the flagship implementation of SHAP on the boston dataset:

```python
# ch4_shap_local.py
import xgboost
import shap

X, y = shap.datasets.boston()
model = xgboost.XGBRegressor().fit(X, y)

explainer = shap.Explainer(model)
shap_values = explainer(X)

shap.plots.waterfall(shap_values[0])
```

This gives the graph :

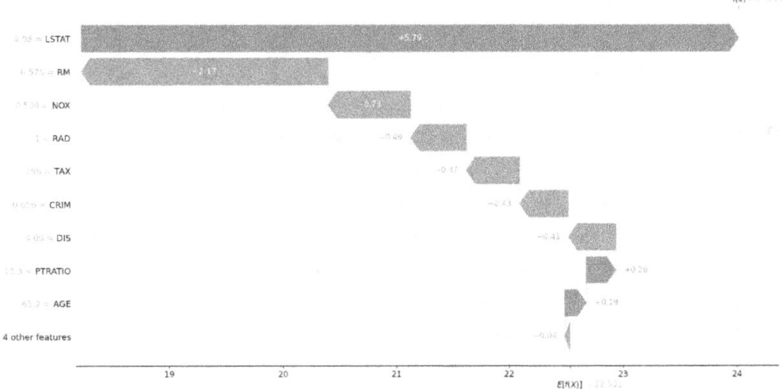

The reading is done from the bottom of the graph, starting from the average value of the values to be predicted. By moving up the features in reverse order of their Shapley value, this base value is progressively modified, until arriving at the predicted value.

The graph confirms the intuitions provided by the classical importance feature, but precisely for the first observation, and adding the crucial information of the sign of the change.

## Overall explainability

The overall explainability is done by aggregating the Shapley values for each observation in the training dataset.

Here again, several representations are possible. This listing using the shap library shows a compact visualization:

```python
# ch4_shap_global.py
import xgboost
import shap
from matplotlib import pyplot as plt

X, y = shap.datasets.boston()
model = xgboost.XGBRegressor().fit(X, y)

explainer = shap.Explainer(model)
shap_values = explainer(X)

shap.plots.beeswarm(shap_values)
plt.show()
```

It allows you to see the whole model at a glance:

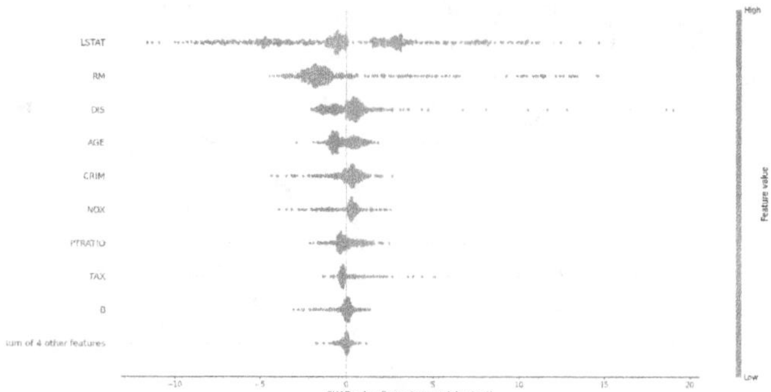


In this case, this shows that the LSTAT feature has a relatively balanced effect on prediction, increasing it globally as much as it reduces it. Its impact is also quite variable in amplitude.

The MR effect, on the other hand, is concentrated around a negative value, within a fairly compact cluster.

# Chapter 6

# Hyper Parameters Tuning

## 6.1 Principles

The previous chapters have shown that building a set of decision trees requires an experimented data scientist. Maximum depth, number of trees, minimum number of points per leaf, regularization parameter, learning rate, ... the list of parameters to configure automatically is long. The risk of obtaining a sub-optimal model following a bad choice is not negligible.

This chapter will first review off-the-shelf methods for automatically testing hyperparameter configurations.

It will then go through the main hyperparameters that need to be set appropriately, showing their impact on the generated models.

Then, a section will present the major libraries implementing more or less advanced algorithms for the search for the optimal set of hyperparameters for a given problem.

The penultimate section will be the occasion to strengthen the understanding of this crucial subject, by detailing the implementation of a Hyper Parameters Tuning algorithm based on XGBoost.

Finally, the link between Hyper Parameter Tuning and AutoML will be discussed.

### 6.1.1 Motivations

The role of hyper-parameter optimization methods is precisely to explore the configuration space formed by all these parameters and to find the best combination as quickly as possible.

This automation offers two benefits for the data scientist: time savings in the development of his model and the guarantee of converging towards an optimal model, unbiased by human intervention.

## 6.1.2   Operation

The underlying principle of hyper-parameter optimization methods is to explore the configuration space and converge as quickly as possible to the optimal combination for a particular criterion.

This criterion is not necessarily the same function as the objective method used to optimize the weights through gradient boosting. It can be any other indicator, and in particular, it is not required that this indicator be derivable. Any function returning a scalar can work.

The difficulty lies in the combinatorics to be explored, which is very large. It is common to find training sessions where the space to be explored extends over :

- Depth from 3 to 10 levels

- A number of trees ranging from 5 to 500

- Gamma ranging from 0.1 to 10

- A learning rate ranging from 0.1 to 1.

- ...

The Cartesian product of all these possibilities is well over 100,000 possibilities. An exploration by brute force, testing all the encountered combinations is in rare cases possible, but in most situations, it is necessary to resort to more intelligent methods. This is all the more true when the training dataset is large and the learning time is long.

## 6.1.3   Available methods

### Brute force

The first possible method, mentioned above, is the brute force method. It simply consists in testing all the possible combinations and keeping the one giving the optimal criterion.

Limited to cases where the configuration space is small, this type of method is called Grid Search. Scikit learn offers a generic method that implements this strategy: GridSearchCV.

> ☞ The suffix CV which is found at the end of the name of the optimization methods of the hyperparameters indicates that the evaluation of the criterion to be optimized is done according to the method of Cross-Validation, namely by calculating it on several datasets.
>
> The more this number of datasets is important, the more the value of the criterion calculated by averaging the scores obtained on these datasets will be close to the theoretical value.

### HalvingGridSearch

A variant of the brute force method is to perform the search by working on an increasingly large number of samples. In the first iteration, all combinatorics are evaluated on a small subset of the data.

In each subsequent iteration, only half of the best-performing combinations are kept while at the same time the number of rows of data is doubled. Iterations continue in this way until all the data has been used or only one combination remains.

This strategy is found in the scikit learn library under the HalvingGridSearchCV class.

Its main advantage lies in the time saving it brings, by quickly discarding the least promising combinations by working on few data.

### Chance

When each training is expensive in terms of computation time, the systematic exploration of all the combinations can be impractical, or restrict the set of parameters to be explored and thus burden the potential of the model.

In this case, it is possible to rely on chance to explore combinatorics. This does not guarantee that the best combination will be retained, but it allows us to keep control of the number of iterations and the computation time.

The RandomizedSearchCV class of scikit learns implements this strategy, and HalvingRandomSearchCV introduces a random search in the previous approach.

### Model-based approach

Relying on randomness may seem surprising, but in practice, it usually results in a satisfactory set of hyperparameters at a low cost.

Nevertheless, it is still possible to miss a configuration that is particularly beneficial for the model under consideration.

Ideally, this should be done in a non-exhaustive way, as the randomized approach does, but with the search guided towards the most promising combinations.

This is what optimization methods based on the use of a surrogate do. The principle is to build a model that can predict the score associated with a configuration of hyperparameters. Different types of underlying models are possible.

These can be Gaussian Mixture models, RandomForest models, or decision trees trained with gradient boosting.

An implementation for this type of method, based on XGBoost, will be given in the rest of this chapter.

Hyperopt, Raytune, SMAC, GpyOpt, and skopt are all libraries that implement this type of approach, which are particularly effective in practice.

## 6.2   Hyper parameters

### 6.2.1   Definition

As shown in the chapter on how Gradient Boosting works, when training a decision tree with a gradient boosting method, only the weights associated with the leaves and the decision criteria are learned.

The structure of the tree, i.e. its maximum depth and the number of estimators are fixed in advance, according to the choice of the data scientist.

These values, as well as the minimum number of samples per leaf, are quite crucial in the final performance of the model.

These types of parameters, which do not evolve during the learning process, are called hyperparameters.

It is therefore essential to understand the role of these parameters at different levels. First, they have an impact on the structure of the generated tree forest. Secondly, they influence the learning time of the model, i.e. the computing power required to train them.

And finally, and this is the key point, they govern the performance of the final model.

The following sections will detail each of these hyperparameters, to understand what value to give them to obtain a model that meets a particular need.

> ☞ It is important to note that even if the hyperparameters
> are common to most of the gradient-boosting imple-
> mentations for decision trees, each library can propose
> additional parameters. This chapter will present the
> main ones.

### 6.2.2  Structural parameters

#### Number of estimators

The first hyperparameter to consider when configuring the training of a decision tree forest is the number of estimators.

This number indicates how many trees will be trained, sequentially and incrementally, to build the final strong predictor.

The reasoning behind the choice of the value of this parameter is based on the notion of bias/variance trade-off, mentioned above. As a reminder, this trade-off is at the heart of any modeling approach and concerns the place where the cursor is positioned between a simple but systematically biased model and a complex but probably overfitted model for a set of data.

Applied to the determination of the number of estimators, this principle amounts to choosing a number large enough to capture the variability of the data while avoiding overfitting.

Identifying the right value is not easy at first. It depends on the complexity of the phenomenon to be modeled. The most reliable way to fix this parameter is to proceed to several trainings, by methodically evaluating the performances on the training dataset and the test dataset. These multiple trainings can be done sequentially, manually, or automated by coupling cross-validation and optimization of the hyperparameters.

In a very general way, the value of this parameter is around 150 for datasets whose cardinality is close to one million lines.

Smaller values are sometimes found for systems that are simple to predict or classify. Larger values, exceeding thousands, are to be reserved for very complex models, with a large number of columns or rows and are often a sign of overfitting.

#### Maximum depth

The other parameter to be taken into account to influence the structure of the learned trees is the maximum depth.

It simply indicates the maximum depth that a tree can reach. It is a maximum, which may not be reached, if the number of samples is not sufficient to add an extra stage, or if the gain is not sufficient.

The maximum depth therefore indirectly controls the number of nodes in the tree and more importantly the number of leaves.

In addition to being a dimensioning parameter for the structure of the trees, it should be related to the number of data used for training. Since decision trees are almost systematically binary trees, a depth of n levels imposes a number of leaves of $2^n$.

The calculation of the weights associated with a leaf is based on the samples of data present in this leaf, so a minimum of $2^{n-1}$ data is required to train a tree of depth n.

The following code snippet illustrates this link between tree depth and the number of leaves. It builds a predictor using XG-Boost that must learn to double the numbers from 1 to 4, and quadruple the numbers from 5 to 9.

Our training set, therefore, contains 9 inputs, each with a different output. The tree resulting from the training should therefore contain 9 leaves. The maximum useful depth is therefore n such that $2^n > 8 = 2^3$ , i.e. n = 4.

```python
import pandas as pd
from xgboost import XGBRegressor

from xgboost import plot_tree
import matplotlib.pyplot as plt

x_train = pd.DataFrame({"A" : [1.0, 2.0, 3.0, 4.0, 5.0,
    6.0, 7.0, 9.0]})
y_train = pd.DataFrame({"Y" : [2.0, 4.0, 6.0, 8.0,
    20.0, 24.0, 28.0, 36.0]})

model = XGBRegressor(n_estimators=1,
                learning_rate=1.,
                base_score=0,
                max_depth=3,
                gamma=0,
                reg_alpha=0,
                reg_lambda=0)

model.fit(x_train, y_train['Y'])
pred = model.predict(x_train)
print(pred) # -> [ 2.  4.  6.  8.  22.  22.  28.  36.]
```

> ☞ The example presented here was chosen to highlight the impact of the maximum depth on the structure of the generated tree.
>
> The regularization hyperparameters have been purposely set to zero, to obtain an accurate prediction. On a real dataset, this should be avoided, in order not to overfit.

This first model, having only a depth n = 3, does not allow complete learning, and does not provide an exact prediction. The decision tree obtained is as follows:

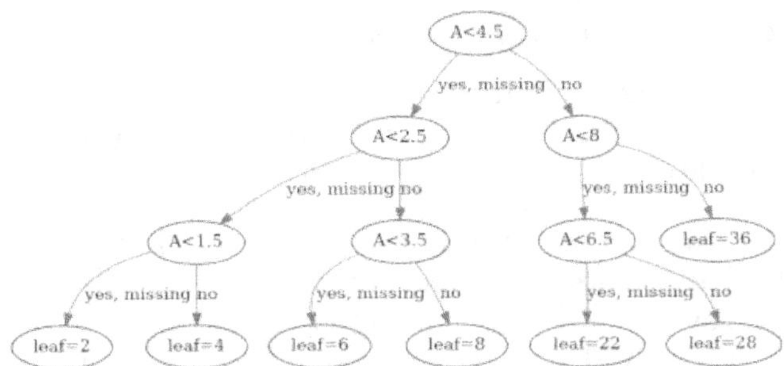

The second model below, whose depth has been increased to 4, and which can therefore predict up to 16 different values, generates the expected predictions.

```python
model = XGBRegressor(n_estimators=1,
                     learning_rate=1.,
                     base_score=0,
                     max_depth=4,
                     gamma=0,
                     reg_alpha=0,
                     reg_lambda=0)

model.fit(x_train, y_train['Y'])
pred = model.predict(x_train)
print(pred) # -> [ 2.  4.  6.  8.  20.  24.  28.  36.]
```

The generated tree contains the right number of leaves, with the right values:

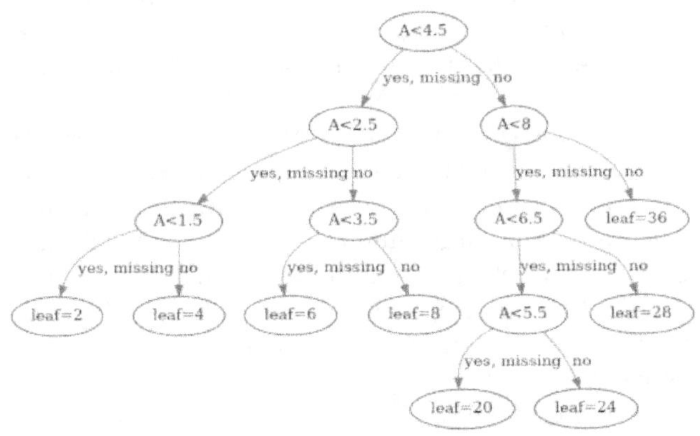

### 6.2.3  Learning parameters

In addition to the hyper-parameters governing the construction of
decision trees, there are a series of parameters that affect learning.

**Impact of learning parameters**

When considering a training parameter, it is important to identify
at which stage of the decision tree construction it comes into play.
Two possibilities are to be considered:

1. The parameter is used to calculate the gain. As a reminder,
   the gain quantifies the interest in adding a new stage to the
   decision tree. A high gain will motivate this addition, while
   a low gain will stop the expansion of the tree. The impact,
   in this case, is therefore structural.

2. The parameter is used to calculate the optimal weight attached to each leaf of the tree. The impact is therefore directly on the correction that will be made. It is therefore
   directly the prediction that will be affected.

Note that these two possibilities are not mutually exclusive.
Certain parameters can influence these two steps.

**Learning rate**

The learning rate is a value between 0 and 1. It allows us to quantify which fraction of the correction will be taken into account.
Consequently, it is a parameter corresponding to the second possibility listed above, and which will immediately influence the predicted value.

This means that the weight calculated using the formulas given
in the chapter on the operation of Gradient Boosting will be multiplied by this learning rate. If it is zero, no correction is applied,
and the model learns nothing.

On the other hand, if this rate is set to 1, the correction is
applied in full.

The purpose of this learning rate is to avoid overfitting, by
transferring only part of the calculated optimal weight. A compromise must therefore be found between a learning rate that is too
small, which implies a larger number of estimators, and a learning
rate close to 1.0, which risks leading to overfitting.

The lines of code below train two models. The first one has a
learning rate of 1 and performs exact learning.

The second has a learning rate of 0.8 and makes predictions
that have been multiplied by 0.8.

```python
import pandas as pd
from xgboost import XGBRegressor

from xgboost import plot_tree
import matplotlib.pyplot as plt

x_train = pd.DataFrame({"A" : [3.0, 2.0, 1.0, 4.0, 5.0,
    6.0, 7.0]})
y_train = pd.DataFrame({"Y" : [3.0, 2.0, 1.0, 4.0, 5.0,
    6.0, 7.0]})

model = XGBRegressor(n_estimators=1,
                     learning_rate=1.,
                     base_score=0,
                     max_depth=3,
                     gamma=0,
                     reg_alpha=0,
                     reg_lambda=0)

model.fit(x_train, y_train['Y'])
pred = model.predict(x_train)
print(pred) # -> [3.0 2.0 1.0 4.0 5.0 6.0 7.0]

model = XGBRegressor(n_estimators=1,
                     learning_rate=1.,
                     base_score=0,
                     max_depth=3,
                     gamma=0,
                     reg_alpha=0,
                     reg_lambda=0)

model.fit(x_train, y_train['Y'])
pred = model.predict(x_train)
print(pred) # -> [2.4 1.6 0.8 3.2 4.  4.8 5.6]
```

The decision tree for this first model shows unmodified weights:

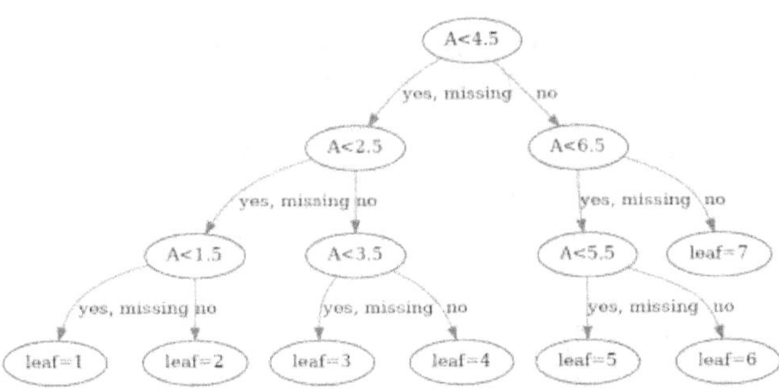


While the second one sees all the weights associated with the leaves multiplied by 0.8 :

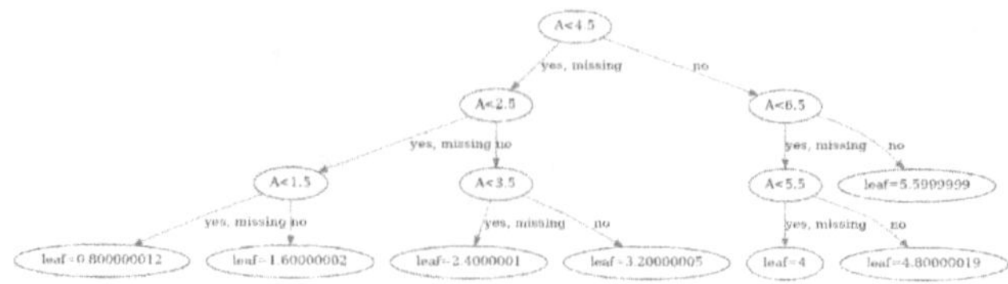

To ensure better accuracy, more trees should be added in this case.

## Gamma regulation parameter

Gamma, as seen in the chapter on the functioning of Gradient Boosting methods, is a regularization parameter of the generated models. That is to say that it governs the learning of decision trees and drives in particular the addition of new nodes based on the gain provided. The reason is given by the following formula, which details the calculation of the optimal gain:

$$\text{Gain} = 1/2 \left[ \frac{G_L^2}{H_L+\lambda} + \frac{G_R^2}{H_R+\lambda} - \frac{(G_L+G_R)^2}{H_L+H_R+\lambda} \right] - \gamma$$

This gain shows the gradient G, the hessian H, T the number of leaves of the tree, the lambda parameter, and finally gamma, and this for the new right (R) and left (L) nodes.

The latter is calculated for each possibility of data splitting criteria associated with the parent node. The best criterion is the one that brings the most gain.

The role of gamma is revealed thanks to this formula for the gain. If the payoff without the regularization is less than gamma, then it is negative, and therefore will not be retained.

This parameter is therefore likely to modify the structure of the generated tree.

Playing with gamma means controlling how easily a node is split in two. If gamma is zero, splitting occurs automatically. With a gamma value strictly greater than zero, splitting only takes place if the generated gain exceeds this threshold.

The following code, using XGBoost, clarifies this operation in the context of classifying an integer as positive or not:

```python
# hp_xgb_gamma.py
import pandas as pd
import numpy as np
from xgboost import XGBRegressor

x_train = pd.DataFrame({"A" : [-3.0, -2.0, -1.0, 0.0,
    1.0, 2.0, 3.0]})
```

```python
y_train = pd.DataFrame({"Y" : [-1, -1, -1, 1.0, 1.0,
    1.0, 1.0]})
y_train['Y'] = y_train['Y'] + np.random.normal(0, .1,
    y_train.shape[0])

# overfitting
model = XGBRegressor(n_estimators=1,
                     learning_rate=1.,
                     base_score=0,
                     max_depth=3,
                     gamma=0,
                     reg_alpha=0,
                     reg_lambda=0)

model.fit(x_train, y_train['Y'])
pred = model.predict(x_train)
print(pred) # -> [-1.1452967 -0.9385602 -0.82778156
    0.9230837 1.0179658 1.2299678 1.0467842 ]

# regularization
model = XGBRegressor(n_estimators=1,
                     learning_rate=1.,
                     base_score=0,
                     max_depth=3,
                     gamma=1,
                     reg_alpha=0,
                     reg_lambda=0)

model.fit(x_train, y_train['Y'])
pred = model.predict(x_train)
print(pred) # -> [-0.9705461 -0.9705461 -0.9705461
    1.0544504 1.0544504 1.0544504 1.0544504]
```

The training data associate the label -1 to strictly negative integers, and 1 to positive or zero integers. Gaussian noise is added to make this school case more realistic and to allow overfitting.

The first training has a gamma value of 0. There is nothing to prevent overfitting during the training. This is what happens as shown by the prediction obtained, which generates seven different values and as many leaves, whereas two would be sufficient.

The tree constructed confirms this first analysis:

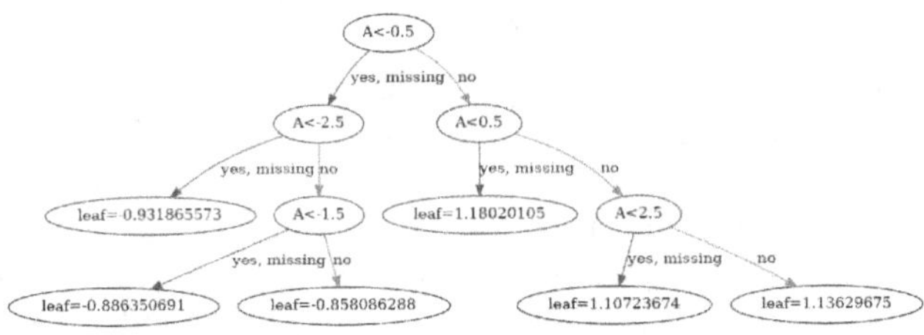

The second test uses a gamma value of 1.  The addition of a new level to the tree is therefore only done if the gain brought by this cutting exceeds 1.

The predictions obtained confirm that this strategy is the right one, since only two labels, -0.9705461 1.0544504, are associated with the different values. Visualizing the constructed tree supports this result:

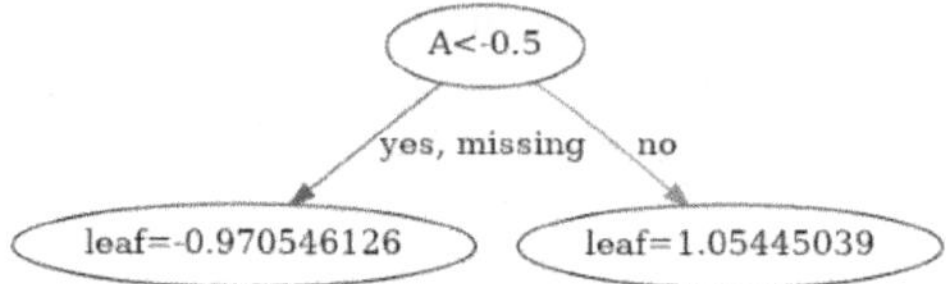


The resulting model captured the essence of the problem at hand: classifying integers into two categories, according to whether they are positive or negative.

Playing with gamma did help to avoid overfitting by modulating the learned structure.

## L2 type regulation parameter: lambda

The second parameter that appears in the formula giving the gain from cutting a node and adding two new leaves is lambda. As the above formula reminds us, the impact of lambda is in the denominator of the gain, where it is summed to H, which is the sum of the Hessians.

More precisely, lambda is found in the expression computing the optimal weight of a leaf :

$$w_j^* = -\frac{G_j}{H_j + \lambda}$$

It is a parameter that will play on both sides: the steering of the decision tree structure, through its intervention in the calculation of the gain; the predicted value through its intervention in the calculation of the weight of a leaf.

However, as seen in the chapter on the operation of gradient boosting methods for decision trees, when the loss function is the squared error, the Hessian is 2. H is therefore twice the number of lines belonging to the current node.

Adding lambda to this value, which is in the denominator, reduces the gain, especially since the number of samples associated with this node is small. Indeed, the more data points are attached to this node, the more the impact of lambda becomes negligible.

At the same time, lambda will also affect the weight attached to the sheet in question, tending to reduce this value the more the number of samples in it is reduced. This is an interesting result since a leaf containing a few data from the training will ultimately have a moderate effect on the prediction.

> ☞ Lambda is often referred to as L2 regularization. This means that it intervenes on the terms of the second degree of the objective function, here the square of the weights. The formula is given below.

$$\Omega(f) = \gamma T + \frac{1}{2}\lambda \sum_{j=1}^{T} w_j^2$$

The code below highlights the impact of lambda on the generated tree:

```python
# hp_xgb_lambda.py
import pandas as pd
import numpy as np
from xgboost import XGBRegressor

x_train = pd.DataFrame({"A" : [-3.0, -2.0, -1.0, 0.0,
    1.0, 2.0, 3.0]})
y_train = pd.DataFrame({"Y" : [-1, -1, -1, 1.0, 1.0,
    1.0, 1.0]})
y_train['Y'] = y_train['Y'] + np.random.normal(0, .1,
    y_train.shape[0])

# overfitting
model = XGBRegressor(n_estimators=1,
                     learning_rate=1.,
                     base_score=0,
                     max_depth=3,
                     gamma=0,
                     reg_alpha=0,
                     reg_lambda=0)

model.fit(x_train, y_train['Y'])
pred = model.predict(x_train)
print(pred) # -> [-1.1452967 -0.9385602 -0.82778156
    0.9230837 1.0179658 1.2299678 1.0467842 ]
```

It is always a question of classifying integers according to their sign, and the first model, with lambda at zero, clearly overfits. Each entry has its own label where two would have been enough.

```python
# regularization
model = XGBRegressor(n_estimators=1,
                     learning_rate=1.,
                     base_score=0,
                     max_depth=3,
                     gamma=0,
                     reg_alpha=1,
                     reg_lambda=0)

model.fit(x_train, y_train['Y'])
pred = model.predict(x_train)
print(pred) # -> [-0.62654 -0.62654 -0.62654 0.77346283
    0.77346283 0.77346283]
```

the second one, with lambda being 1, allows to limit this overfitting, and ensures the creation of a model with 2 leaves, as expected. The constructed tree is as expected:

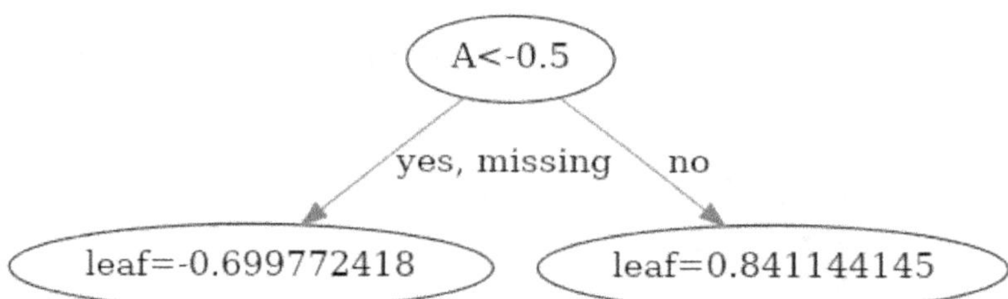


The lambda parameter has affected the structure of the tree. It is important to note that the weights of the leaves have smaller values than with a regularization with gamma. This is the limiting effect on the magnitude of the square of the weights, which tends to limit the absolute values of the weights.

A third training, this time with five times as much data, has, as the formula suggested, a smaller impact on the weights, since there is more data per node:

```python
# regularization of more data
x_train = pd.DataFrame({"A" : [-3.0, -2.0, -1.0, 0.0,
    1.0, 2.0, 3.0] * 10})
y_train = pd.DataFrame({"Y" : [-1, -1, -1, 1.0, 1.0,
    1.0, 1.0] * 10})
y_train['Y'] = y_train['Y'] + np.random.normal(0, .1,
    y_train.shape[0])

model = XGBRegressor(n_estimators=1,
                     learning_rate=1.,
```

```
                base_score=0,
                max_depth=3,
                gamma=0,
                reg_alpha=1,
                reg_lambda=0)

model.fit(x_train, y_train['Y'])
pred = model.predict(x_train)
print(pred) # -> [-0.9705461 -0.9705461 -0.9705461
      1.0544504 1.0544504 1.0544504 1.0544504]
```

Again, the learned tree has two leaves, this time with weights less constrained in value, and thus very close to the expected values -1 and 1 :

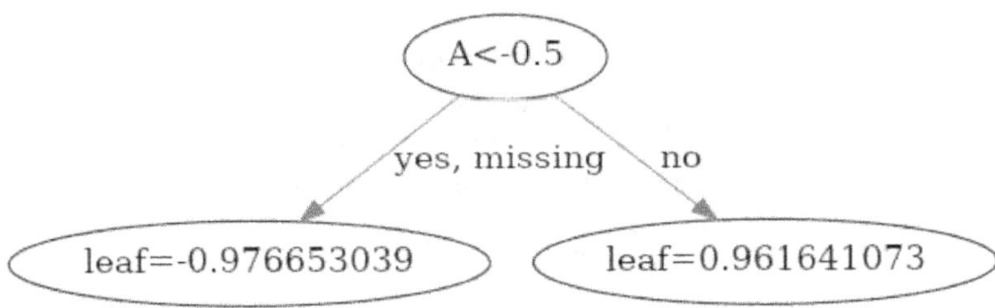


This behavior is to be compared with what would be obtained by using gamma for regularization, again in the case where the number of training data is multiplied by 5:

```
model = XGBRegressor(n_estimators=1,
                learning_rate=1.,
                base_score=0,
                max_depth=3,
                gamma=1,
                reg_alpha=0,
                reg_lambda=0)

model.fit(x_train, y_train['Y'])
pred = model.predict(x_train)
print(pred) # -> -0.9960624 -0.9960624 -0.9960624
      0.99365574 0.99365574 0.99365574 ...
```

The weights remain closer to 1 :

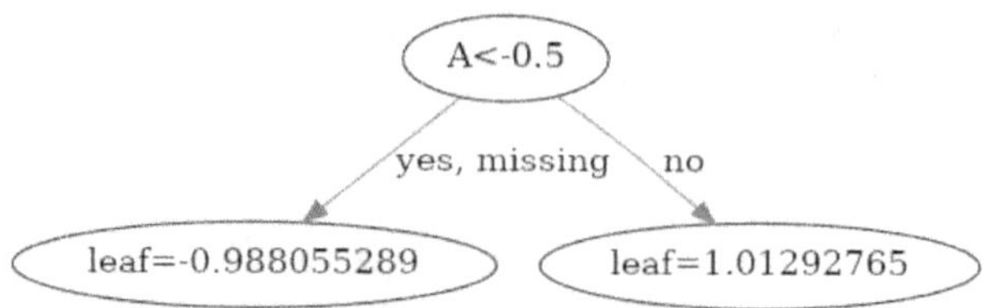


In general, since lambda forces weight values to remain small for small amounts of attached data, this implies that the corrections made by each leaf are limited. A non-zero lambda value, therefore, favors a larger number of leaves and trees for the same level of accuracy.

## L1 type regulation parameter: alpha

In the same way as lambda, there is another parameter defined to natively influence the value of the weights. It is generally noted alpha and involves the sum of the absolute value of the weights in the regularization function.

> ☞ In parallel to lambda, which performs an L2 type regularization, since it applies to the square of the weights, alpha performs an L1 type regularization since it applies to the absolute values of the weights.

As such, alpha has a joint effect on the structure of the tree, by influencing the gain, but also the weight of the leaves.

The L1 regularization has the consequence to add alpha to the weight when it is negative, and removing alpha when it is positive. This means that it tends towards zero.

This behavior tends to generate sparse models, i.e. models where a maximum of weights tend to be zero.

The following code highlights this, by generating two models for the well-known textbook case of iris classification.

The first one uses an L2-type regularization, by imposing a value of 2 on lambda. The second one applies an L1-type regularization, by forcing the value of alpha to 2.

```python
# hp_xgb_alpha.py
import numpy as np
from sklearn import datasets
from sklearn.model_selection import train_test_split
from sklearn.metrics import precision_score
from sklearn.metrics import confusion_matrix

from xgboost import XGBClassifier
import matplotlib.pyplot as plt

iris = datasets.load_iris()
X = iris.data
y = iris.target

X_train, X_test, y_train, y_test = train_test_split(X,
    y, test_size=0.2, random_state=42)

# L2 type regulation
model = XGBClassifier(n_estimators=20,
                      learning_rate=0.3,
                      max_depth=3,
                      gamma=0,
                      reg_alpha=0,
                      reg_lambda=2,
                      eval_metric='mlogloss',
                      use_label_encoder=False,
                      num_class=3)

model.fit(X_train, y_train)
preds = model.predict(X_test)
print(confusion_matrix(y_test, preds))
# -> [[10 0 0]
# -> [ 0 9 0]
# -> [ 0 0 11]]

# weight recovery
dtf = model.get_booster().trees_to_dataframe()
dtf = dtf[dtf.Feature == 'Leaf']
# recovery of weights close to zero
dtf = dtf.sort_values(by=['Tree', 'Node', 'Gain'])
print('zero weights:', dtf[abs(dtf.Gain) == 0].shape) #
    -> zero weights: (0, 10)

# L1 type regulation - sparse model
model = XGBClassifier(n_estimators=20,
                      learning_rate=0.3,
                      max_depth=3,
```

```python
                            gamma=0,
                            reg_alpha=2,
                            reg_lambda=0,
                            eval_metric='mlogloss',
                            use_label_encoder=False,
                            num_class=3)

model.fit(X_train, y_train)
preds = model.predict(X_test)
print(confusion_matrix(y_test, preds))
# -> [[10 0 0]
# -> [ 0 9 0]
# -> [ 0 0 11]]
# weight recovery
dtf = model.get_booster().trees_to_dataframe()
dtf = dtf[dtf.Feature == 'Leaf']
# recovery of weights close to zero
dtf = dtf.sort_values(by=['Tree', 'Node', 'Gain'])
print('zero weights:', dtf[abs(dtf.Gain) == 0].shape) #
    -> zero weights: (65, 10)
```

In the first case, we were asked to display the number of nodes whose weight is zero. There are none.

The same exercise is performed for the second model. This time, 65 weights have exactly zero value.

The following two curves plot the weights of each leaf, for both models, in descending order:

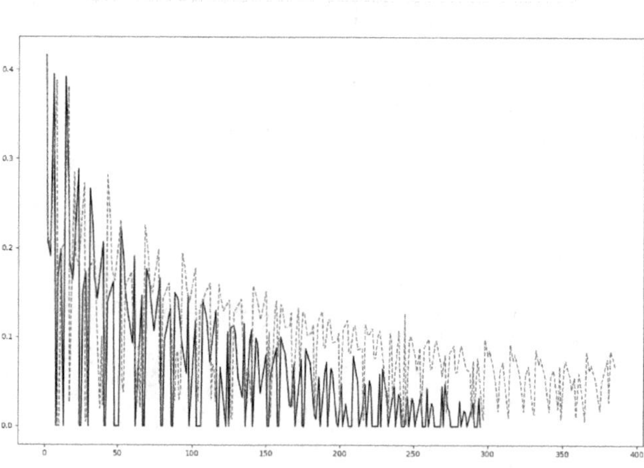


The model with L1 regularization uses far fewer non-zero weights, and also uses values closer to zero.

Using an L1 regularization, taking a positive alpha value, produces the effect predicted by the mathematical theory: the resulting model is much deeper than the model with L2 regularization.

The comparison of the obtained trees confirms again the behavior of alpha. With alpha equal to 2, the generated trees contain zeros. Example with the fifth estimator :

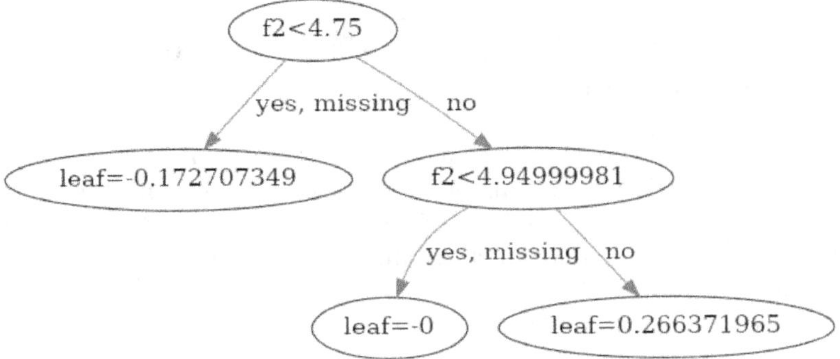

This is not the case when lambda is equal to 2:

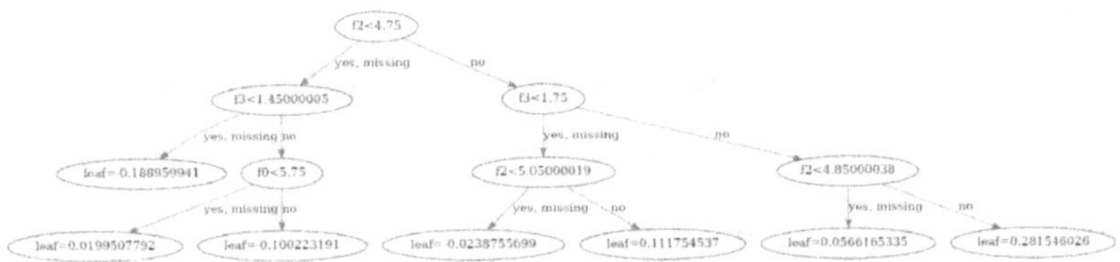

> ☞ In numerical analysis, the adjective sparse, describing systems with many zeros, arises from the fact that the zeros are not stored in the corresponding matrices. The latter is then essentially empty, hence the sparce adjective.

The confusion matrices obtained in both cases are the same. Each model correctly identifies the correct class associated with a sample, without ever confusing one category with another.

So they are both equally effective. So why favor a sparse model over a dense one?

Two motivations can govern this choice. The first one, less important from a Data Science point of view, is nevertheless worth mentioning: the resulting model being sparse, contains a lot of zeros, which it is possible not to store. For large models, this can be a significant storage gain.

The second is that by concentrating most of the information on leaves for which the weight will not be zero, L1 regularizations perform a form of selection of the discriminating characteristics: this is feature selection.

This step is sometimes performed before training the model, but by selecting this type of regularization, it is possible to do without it, which simplifies the task.

## 6.3   Existing Libraries for Hyper Parameter Optimization

As shown in the previous sections, which presented in a non-exhaustive way the major hyper-parameters to be taken into account, the combinatorics to be explored to configure a model can quickly become large. It is tedious, unproductive, and often impossible to manually evaluate all the possibilities.

The first section of this chapter presented the main types of methods that can be used to automate this exploration.

This new section lists and details some of the most popular libraries for automating this search.

All of them provide a solution to the following problem: finding the optimal combination of parameters concerning a precise and quantified objective. Each one proposes a different strategy to achieve it.

### 6.3.1   Scikit-learn

Scikit-learn is the reference toolbox for data scientists working in python. It covers many domains, from classification to regression, through dimension reduction, data pre-processing, and clustering. It implements of course hyperparameter selection methods.

These are not among the most advanced and are derivatives of the brute force methods presented at the beginning of this chapter.

They will not be suitable for modeling where the volume and/or complexity of the data leads to long training times. On the other hand, in simpler cases, their exhaustive character can be interesting.

The few lines below give an example of the use of GridSearchCV, which performs an exhaustive search by brute force:

```python
from sklearn import svm, datasets
from sklearn.model_selection import GridSearchCV

iris = datasets.load_iris()
parameters = { 'kernel':('linear', 'rbf'), 'C':[1, 10]}
svc = svm.SVC()
```

```
clf = GridSearchCV(svc, parameters)
clf.fit(iris.data, iris.target)
print(clf.best_params_)
#  'C': 1, 'kernel':  'linear'
```

## 6.3.2 Scikit-optimize

Scikit-optimize is a library that allows one to search for the optimal combination of parameters with respect to an objective function. It is thus a generic library that can be applied to other things than the search for the hyperparameters generating the best model.

In the case studied in this book, the function to be maximized or minimized must measure how well the model under consideration is performing. It can be an error metric, like the mean absolute error, MAE, or the mean relative error, MAPE. But it can also be a metric calculating the precision or the relevance of the model, such as the r2 criterion.

> ☞ It is important to remember here that the objective function optimized during the search for the best hyperparameters can be different from the one used for the calculation of the weights with the Gradient Boosting.
>
> In particular, there is no requirement that it be derivable. However, it is necessary to ensure consistency between these two objectives.

The strategy adopted by scikit-optimize is the surrogate approach, described in the first part of this chapter. It is based on various types of models, such as Gaussian Processes or Random Forest.

These underlying models are trained as you explore, and are responsible for predicting the gain associated with a given configuration.

The usage is quite similar to scikit, as the following listing shows:

```
from sklearn import svm, datasets
from skopt import BayesSearchCV

iris = datasets.load_iris()
parameters = { 'kernel':('linear', 'rbf'), 'C':[1, 10]}
svc = svm.SVC()
clf = BayesSearchCV(svc, parameters)
clf.fit(iris.data, iris.target)
print(clf.best_params_)
# OrderedDict([('C', 8), ('kernel', 'rbf')])
```

In this example, the search is guided by a Bayesian model.

## 6.3.3   SMAC

SMAC is another example of a library allowing this search for the optimal set of hyperparameters. Like scikit-optimize, it relies on the principle of a sub-model to evaluate the relevance of a combination of hyper-parameters at a low cost.

It supports only one type of submodel: random forests.

Its use requires a few more lines of code than the solutions seen above:

```python
import numpy as np

from ConfigSpace.hyperparameters import
    UniformFloatHyperparameter,
    UniformIntegerHyperparameter

import xgboost as xgb

from sklearn.model_selection import cross_val_score
from sklearn import datasets

from smac.configspace import ConfigurationSpace
from smac.facade.smac_hpo_facade import SMAC4HPO
from smac.scenario.scenario import Scenario


iris = datasets.load_iris()

def xgboost_from_cfg(cfg):
    clf = xgb.XGBClassifier(**cfg, random_state=0)
    scores = cross_val_score(clf, iris.data, iris.
        target)
    return 1 - np.mean(scores)

cs = ConfigurationSpace()

max_depth = UniformIntegerHyperparameter("max_depth",
    1, 10, default_value=3)
cs.add_hyperparameter(max_depth)

learning_rate = UniformFloatHyperparameter("
    learning_rate", 0.01, 1.0, default_value=1.0, log=
    True)
cs.add_hyperparameter(learning_rate)

max_features = UniformIntegerHyperparameter("gamma", 0,
    10, default_value=4)
cs.add_hyperparameters([max_features])
```

```python
scenario = Scenario({"run_obj": "quality",
                     "runcount-limit": 10,
                     "cs": cs,
                     "deterministic": "true",
                     "wallclock_limit": 120})

smac = SMAC4HPO(scenario=scenario, rng=np.random.
    RandomState(0), tae_runner=xgboost_from_cfg)

incumbent = smac.optimize()

print(incumbent)
#Configuration:
# gamma, Value:  1
# learning_rate, Value:  0.01410391335544212192
# max_depth, Value:  7
```

### 6.3.4 Ray tune

The last library of this panel is RayTune. Like SMAC and scikit-optimize it exploits underlying models to quickly select promising configurations.

However, it differs from the two previous ones by focusing its efforts on scalability. Indeed, it allows us to easily distribute the computations on different machines, to be able to process complex models in a reasonable time.

Its design, however, is less generic, and it only allows for optimal hyperparameters.

Its implementation is close to that of SMAC, as the following code shows:

```python
import sklearn.datasets
import sklearn.metrics
from sklearn.model_selection import train_test_split
import xgboost as xgb

from ray import tune


def train_iris(config):
    data, labels = sklearn.datasets.load_iris(
        return_X_y=True)
    train_x, test_x, train_y, test_y = train_test_split
        (
        data, labels, test_size=0.25)
    train_set = xgb.DMatrix(train_x, label=train_y)
    test_set = xgb.DMatrix(test_x, label=test_y)
```

```python
    results = {}
    xgb.train(
        configuring,
        train_set,
        evals=[(test_set, "eval")],
        evals_result=results,
        verbose_eval=False)

    accuracy = 1. - results["eval"]["error"][-1]
    tune.report(mean_accuracy=accuracy, done=True)


config = {
    "eval_metric": [ "logloss", "error" ],
    "max_depth": tune.randint(1, 9),
    "min_child_weight": tune.choice([1, 2, 3]),
    "subsample": tune.uniform(0.5, 1.0),
    "eta": tune.loguniform(1e-4, 1e-1)
}
analysis = tune.run(
    train_iris,
    resources_per_trial={"cpu": 8},
    config=config,
    num_samples=10)

print(analysis.get_best_config(metric="mean_accuracy",
    mode="min"))
#   'eval_metric': ['logloss', 'error'], 'max_depth':
#   3, 'min_child_weight': 2, 'subsample':
#   0.78108576405470034, 'eta':  0.012662938165536894
```

## 6.4 Optimizing XGBoost with XGBoost

### 6.4.1 Objective

This last but one section will be the occasion to see concretely how to implement an efficient hyper-parameter search, based on a surrogate approach. And to stay in the theme of this book and rely on the Gradient Boosting library that has the support of the majority of the Data Scientists community, XGBoost will be used as a surrogate. XGBoost will then be used to optimize Xgboost.

### 6.4.2 General principle

The main idea behind optimization using a surrogate model is to be able to evaluate the suitability of a configuration without having to run a complete training.

The gain is then all the more important as the substitution model quickly and reliably provides this evaluation.

Once this surrogate is available, the general algorithm is simple: n configurations are randomly drawn. The surrogate model performs a gain estimation for each one. The most promising configuration is then actually tested on the model to be trained. The gain obtained is reused to enrich the surrogate model.

This sequence is repeated as many times as necessary, usually a fixed number of times.

### 6.4.3  Configuration space and sampling

There are two prerequisites for finding an optimal hyperparameter configuration:

1. It is necessary to be able to describe this space of exploration

2. It is necessary to be able to sample, that is to say, to draw randomly configurations of this space

Fortunately, there is a library in python that makes it easy: ConfigSpace.

The following few lines clarify its use, starting by adding numerical parameters:

```python
from ConfigSpace import ConfigurationSpace
from ConfigSpace.hyperparameters import
    CategoricalHyperparameter, \
    UniformFloatHyperparameter,
        UniformIntegerHyperparameter

num_trees = UniformIntegerHyperparameter("num_trees",
    10, 50, default_value=10)
max_features = UniformIntegerHyperparameter("
    max_features", 1, 100, default_value=1)
min_weight_frac_leaf = UniformFloatHyperparameter("
    min_weight_frac_leaf", 0.0, 0.5, default_value=0.0)
min_samples_to_split = UniformIntegerHyperparameter("
    min_samples_to_split", 2, 20, default_value=2)
min_samples_in_leaf = UniformIntegerHyperparameter("
    min_samples_in_leaf", 1, 20, default_value=1)
max_leaf_nodes = UniformIntegerHyperparameter("
    max_leaf_nodes", 10, 1000, default_value=100)
```

The definition of the latter requires only their name and their minimum and maximum bounds. Note also that there are different types for integers or reals.

It is also possible to add categorical parameters, as shown in the following lines:

```
do_bootstrapping = CategoricalHyperparameter("
    do_bootstrapping", ["true", "false"], default_value
    ="true")
criterion = CategoricalHyperparameter("criterion", ["
    mse", "mae"], default_value="mse")
```

Finally, all these parameters can be grouped in a configuration space:

```
cs = ConfigurationSpace()
cs.add_hyperparameters([num_trees, min_weight_frac_leaf
    ,
                        max_features,
                            min_samples_to_split,
                        min_samples_in_leaf,
                            max_leaf_nodes, criterion,
                            do_bootstrapping])
```

The latter can then be queried simply to provide a random configuration:

```
cs.sample_configuration()
# > Configuration:
# criterion, Value: 'mae'
# do_bootstrapping, Value: 'false'
# max_features, Value: 36
# max_leaf_nodes, Value: 170
# min_samples_in_leaf, Value: 19
# min_samples_to_split, Value: 9
# min_weight_frac_leaf, Value: 0.018895139352121226
# num_trees, Value: 37
```

### 6.4.4  Optimizer

Once you can generate allowable configurations, you need a way to evaluate them.

The class created below, Optimizer will take care of this:

```
import pandas as pd
import numpy as np


class Optimizer:
    def __init__(self,
                 algo_score,
                 max_iter,
                 max_intensity,
                 model,
                 cs):
        self.traj = []
        self.algo_score = algo_score
        self.max_iter = max_iter
```

```python
        self.max_intensification = max_intensification
        self.internal_model = model()
        self.trajectory = []
        self.cfgs = []
        self.scores = {}
        self.best_cfg = None
        self.best_score = None
        self.cs = cs
```

To build it, we need to pass it a function, algo_score, which will train the model and compute the score at the end of the training. The arguments max_iter and max_intensification respectively set the maximum number of trainings and the maximum number of candidate configurations that will be evaluated by the surrogate model.

The model parameter is a function allowing instantiating the internal model, which will act as a substitute. Finally, cs is the configuration space to explore, as defined in the previous section.

> ☞ To generalize the code of this optimizer, which could be applied to something other than a model training, the core of the process to be optimized is encapsulated in the algo_score method.

The internal model will therefore have the role of estimating the probable score of a configuration. To do this, we have to convert the configuration, which is given in the form of a dictionary key/value, into an array of type dataset pandas. This is what the cfg_to_dtf method does:

```python
def cfg_to_dtf(self, cfgs):
    cfgs = [dict(cfg) for cfg in cfgs]
    dtf = pd.DataFrame(cfgs)
    return dtf
```

Then comes the central part of this class, the optimize method, which will perform the selection of the best configuration. It starts by randomly drawing a first configuration and performing the first run on it, to obtain a first reference score. The score obtained and the configuration are stored for analysis, and the configuration is converted into datasets, to feed the internal model:

```python
def optimize(self):
    cfg = self.cs.sample_configuration()
    self.cfgs.append(cfg)
    self.trajectory.append(cfg)

    score = self.algo_score(cfg)
    self.scores[cfg] = score
```

```python
        self.best_cfg = cfg
        self.best_score = score
        dtf = self.cfg_to_dtf(self.cfgs)
```

It then enters the iteration loop that will work to converge on the best configuration.

Two situations are possible: either this is the first iteration, or there is not enough data to build the internal model. In this case, a new configuration is drawn, evaluated, and added to the training dataset for the substitute model.

Either enough data are available: in this case, the internal model can be trained and applied to select among the randomly drawn candidate configurations the most promising one. The model to be optimized, represented by the algo_score function, is learned in the process with the new configuration. If the score obtained is better than the previous one, the configuration becomes the best.

```python
for i in range(0, self.max_iter):
    if dtf.shape[0] > 1:
        scores = np.array([ val for key, val in
            self.scores.items()])
        self.internal_model.fit(dtf, scores)

        candidates = [self.cs.
            sample_configuration() for i in
            range(0, self.max_intensification)]
        candidate_scores = [self.internal_model.
            predict(self.cfg_to_dtf([cfg])) for
            cfg in candidates]
        best_candidates = np.argmax(
            candidate_scores)

        cfg = candidates[best_candidates]
        self.cfgs.append(cfg)
        score = self.algo_score(cfg)
        self.scores[cfg] = score

        if score > self.best_score:
            self.best_cfg = cfg
            self.best_score = score
            self.trajectory.append(cfg)

        dtf = self.cfg_to_dtf(self.cfgs)
    else:
        cfg = self.cs.sample_configuration()
        self.cfgs.append(cfg)
        score = self.algo_score(cfg)
        self.scores[cfg] = score

        if score > self.best_score:
```

```
            self.best_cfg = cfg
            self.best_score = score
            self.trajectory.append(cfg)
    dtf = self.cfg_to_dtf(self.cfgs)
```

## 6.4.5 Application to the boston dataset

In the data scientist community, there is another dataset widely used to test or demonstrate algorithms. It is the Boston Dataset.

It is a corpus of data that lists the sales prices in various Boston neighborhoods, with for each transaction the characteristics of the sale: neighborhood, the surface of the property, number of floors, ...

The goal of the game is then to determine the selling price of the property knowing these attributes.

The following code shows how our hyper-parameter optimizer manages to find an interesting solution, and how it compares to a brute force approach:

```python
import numpy as np
import pandas as pd
from ConfigSpace import ConfigurationSpace
from ConfigSpace.hyperparameters import
    CategoricalHyperparameter, \
    UniformFloatHyperparameter,
        UniformIntegerHyperparameter
from sklearn.datasets import load_boston
from sklearn.ensemble import RandomForestRegressor
from catboost import CatBoostRegressor
from xgboost.sklearn import XGBRegressor
from sklearn.metrics import make_scorer
from sklearn.model_selection import cross_val_score

import matplotlib.pyplot as plt

from optimizer import Optimizer
After the inevitable series of imports, with notably
    the XGBoost and CatBoost libraries, this little
    program defines the run function, which will train
    and evaluate our price predictor model:

def run(data, target, cfg):
    cfg_dict = {key: cfg[key] for key in cfg}
    rfr = RandomForestRegressor(**cfg_dict)

    def rmse(y, y_pred):
        return np.sqrt(np.mean((y_pred - y) ** 2))
```

```python
    rmse_scorer = make_scorer(rmse, greater_is_better=
        False)
    score = cross_val_score(rfr, data, target, cv=5,
        scoring=rmse_scorer, verbose=0)
    score = np.mean(score)

    return score
```

To highlight the generality of this approach, the model used to handle this price prediction exercise is of the RandomForest type. Once again, any model could be used.

> ☞ To refine the value of the score, the cross-validation method is used here, through the call to the cross_val_score method.
>
> The idea is to compute the score on several test datasets, here 5, built automatically according to the Kfold method.

Next comes the definition of the configuration space to be explored:

```python
num_trees = UniformIntegerHyperparameter("n_estimators"
    , 10, 50, default_value=10)
max_features = UniformIntegerHyperparameter("
    max_features", 1, 13, default_value=1)
min_weight_frac_leaf = UniformFloatHyperparameter("
    min_weight_fraction_leaf", 0.0, 0.5, default_value
    =0.0)
min_samples_to_split = UniformIntegerHyperparameter("
    min_samples_split", 2, 20, default_value=2)
min_samples_in_leaf = UniformIntegerHyperparameter("
    min_samples_leaf", 1, 20, default_value=1)
max_leaf_nodes = UniformIntegerHyperparameter("
    max_leaf_nodes", 10, 1000, default_value=100)

do_bootstrapping = CategoricalHyperparameter("bootstrap
    ", ["true", "false"], default_value="true")
criterion = CategoricalHyperparameter("criterion", ["
    mse", "mae"], default_value="mse")
cs = ConfigurationSpace()
cs.add_hyperparameters([num_trees, min_weight_frac_leaf
    ,
                        max_features,
                            min_samples_to_split,
                        min_samples_in_leaf,
                            max_leaf_nodes,
                        criterion, do_bootstrapping])
```

The latter mixes numerical and categorical parameters.

The rest of the code determines the optimal configuration with the following 3 types of internal models: with CatBoost, with XG-Boost, and with CatBoost without categorical parameters. Indeed, XGBoost does not natively support categorical settings, so this puts XGBoost and CatBoost on an equal footing.

```python
boston = load_boston()
max_intensity = 25

optimizer = Optimizer(lambda cfg: run(boston.data,
    boston.target, cfg),
                      50, 250,
                      lambda: CatBoostRegressor(
                          cat_features=['criterion', '
                          bootstrap']),
                      cs)
optimizer.optimize()


# XGBoost doesn't support categorical parameters
cs = ConfigurationSpace()
cs.add_hyperparameters([num_trees, min_weight_frac_leaf
    ,
                        max_features,
                          min_samples_to_split,
                        min_samples_in_leaf,
                          max_leaf_nodes])
optimizer_xgb = Optimizer(lambda cfg: run(boston.data,
    boston.target, cfg),
                          50, 250,
                          XGBRegressor,
                          cs)
optimizer_xgb.optimize()

optimizer_cat = Optimizer(lambda cfg: run(boston.data,
    boston.target, cfg),
                          50, 250,
                          CatBoostRegressor,
                          cs)
optimizer_cat.optimize()
```

The following curves show the evolution of the score as a function of the number of iterations. They clearly show that the substitution models learn quite quickly which configurations are promising. Of the three models tested, it appears that CatBoost without categorical features does rather better than the other two.

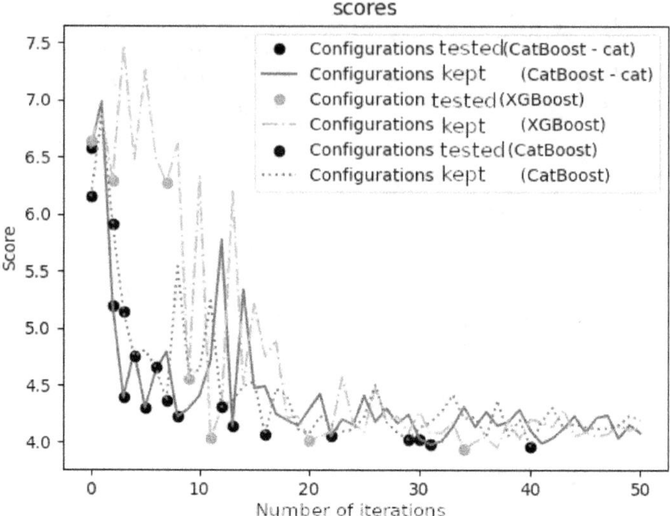


## 6.5    AutoML and Hyper Parameters Tuning

Some tools are starting to propose automation of Machine Learning: it is the autoML. The goal of these tools is to build automatically the best model among several possible ones. The search space is very large: Linear Regression, Logistic Regression, Decision Trees, Vector Machine Support, KNN, ... In this sense, the problem to be solved is very similar to the search for hyperparameters. The methods that have been presented here can be directly applied to this use case.

# Chapter 7

# Using objective functions properly

## 7.1 Rationale for objective functions

Objective functions are central in the construction of decision trees with the Gradient Boosting method.

Indeed, as shown in the second chapter, the whole Gradient Boosting method is based on objective functions.

The choice of the feature retained during the construction of a node is done through the gain, whose calculation derives from the objective function through its gradient and its hessian. Its value is calculated by taking the difference between the current objective of a node and the objectives reached by adding two new nodes. The formula used is the following one:

$$Gain = \frac{1}{2}\left[\frac{G_L^2}{H_L + \lambda} + \frac{G_R^2}{H_R + \lambda} - \frac{(G_L + G_R)^2}{H_L + H_R + \lambda}\right] - \gamma$$

The role of the objective function is therefore essential for the constitution of a collection of decision trees.

In the same spirit, the objective is the essential actor of the prediction itself, since it defines the value of the weights associated with each leaf. As a reminder, the formula that allows us to calculate them is the following one:

$$w_j^* = -\frac{G_j}{H_j + \lambda}$$

Here again, the objective function is involved through its gradient and its hessian. Mastering objective functions is essential and the purpose of this chapter is to become familiar with them.

The next section will recall the essential character of objective functions. Section 3 will present the most common objective functions for classification as well as regression, while section 4 will present some regularized objectives.

Finally, section 5 will show how to implement custom objective functions to refine the training control of XGBoost models. In particular, the case of using quantile functions for confidence interval prediction will be detailed.

## 7.2    Importance of objective functions

Using a given objective function is not neutral on the performance of a model.

Of course, whatever the chosen objective function, the Gradient Boosting method will be able to generate a model. The performance of this model will be optimal for the chosen hyperparameters and this objective.

However, there is no guarantee that the chosen objective is relevant to the business need. The generated model is therefore optimal from a mathematical point of view, but may well not be relevant to the problem under consideration.

Playing with the choice of the objective function is therefore essential to bring the mathematical world closer to the real world.

---

☞ It is important to remember here the distinction between the objective function and the evaluation metrics.

Evaluation metrics, MAE, MAPE, MSE, ... offer a business view on the model performance, but can rarely be used as an objective function. Indeed, the objective functions must be twice derivable.

---

## 7.3    Usual objectives

The three main Gradient Boosting libraries, XGBoost, CatBoost, and LightGBM all offer a few dozen possibilities as objective function choices.

---

☞ Depending on the implementation, the objective function can be called the loss function.

---

The following sections will present the most used ones, depending on the use case: regression or classification.

## 7.3.1  Classification

Classification requires specific objective functions, due to the discrete nature of the predictions. Unlike regression, the possible output values do not form a continuum, but a discrete set.

This particularity has to be taken into account in the objective functions, especially regarding the double derivability which is necessary for Gradient Boosting.

### Logistics function

The logistic function objective is used for binary classifications. It is actually based on two functions: the sigmoid and the log loss.

The sigmoid is used to "binarize" the output of the prediction. Applied to the raw prediction, it gives it the following shape:

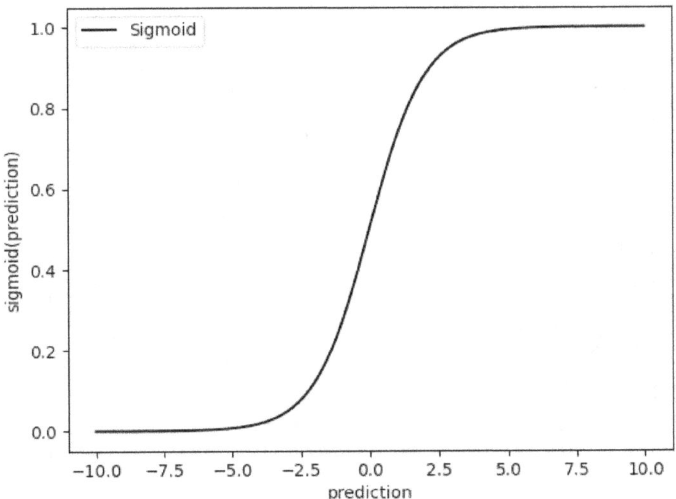

It, therefore, ensures that, outside the transition zone, the output values are indeed 0 or 1.

It is defined by this formula:

$$\sigma(x) = \frac{1}{1 + e^{-x}}$$

The classification is binary, and the sigmoid generates a value in the interval $[0, 1]$, then its output can be considered as the probability to belong to one of these two classes.

This corrected prediction must then be passed to the error function itself. It is not possible in this case to use the square of the error, because the sigmoid function is not linear, and the combination of the two would be non-convex. This means that there are local minima that would prevent convergence to the global minimum.

This is where the log loss comes in, the formula for which is:

$$L_{log}(p) = -(y \cdot log(p) + (1 - y) \cdot log(1 - p))$$

The log loss requires that the prediction p is a probability, which is what the sigmoid provides. Moreover, y is the real class of the considered sample.

This loss function actually contains two functions: if y is 1, then the loss function is -lop(p), while if y is 0, it is -log(1-p). Graphically, this gives:

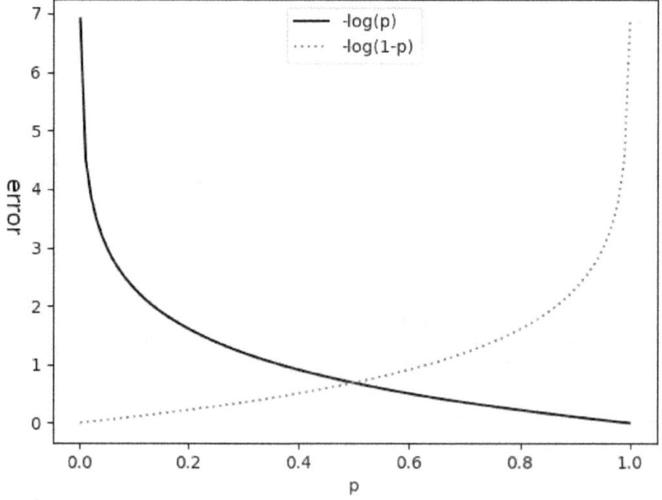


The further the prediction is from the target value, the greater the loss becomes exponentially.

**Soft Max**

In the case where there are strictly more than 2 classes to be used, the approach presented above must be adapted.

The first thing to understand is that it is no longer possible to use a simple real to classify into more than two classes. It is then impossible to use a single collection of decision trees. We need as many trees as there are classes.

Each of its decision trees will therefore predict whether a sample matches to the corresponding class or one of the remaining classes. A prediction then no longer results in a single scalar value, but in a vector of the same dimension as the number of classes.

So we will have to find a function which, in the same way as the sigmoid transforms a scalar into a 0 or a 1, transforms this time the n values of a vector into an integer which indicates the index of the corresponding class.

For this, the softmax function is the ideal candidate. This function will return, for a vector of predictions, the probability for each element of the vector to be the right class.

The class with the highest prediction then becomes the prediction.

## 7.3.2 Regression

Even more than the objective functions for classification, the objective functions for regression have a direct impact on the predictions, due to the continuous nature of this type of prediction.

This section will go into detail about the most frequently used ones.

**Squared error**

By far the most commonly applied, the squared error function is systematically the default value for regression. It is found everywhere in Machine Learning, starting with the least squares method. It is computed as follows:

$$se(\hat{y}, y) = (\hat{y} - y)^2$$

Its popularity stems, in addition to deeper motivations based on physics and the concept of energy, from its simplicity of derivation. Its first derivative is the double of the error, while its second derivative is the constant 2.

Its plot provides information on how it will behave as an objective function:

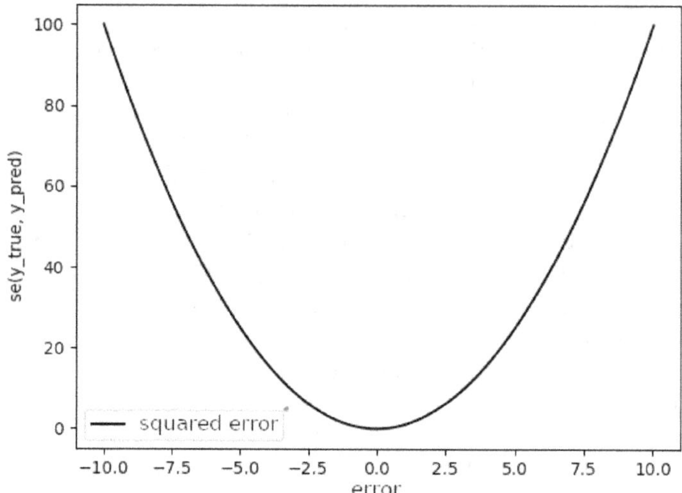

The larger the error, the larger the value it will generate. Doubling the error quadruples the square of the error.

This implies that in its mission of minimizing the objective function, the Gradient Boosting method will focus on the large errors, at the risk of focusing only on the large values.

An error of 100 between an actual value of 1000 and a prediction of 1100 will be considered 100 times more than an error of 10 between an actual value of 15 and a prediction of 25. In percentage terms, the error of 100 for a value of 1000 is less problematic than an error of 10 for an actual value of 15.

## Pseudo Huber Loss

An alternative way to consider errors uniformly, without over-compensating for large errors, would be to use the mean absolute error.

Unfortunately, this metric is not derivable. It is therefore not possible to compute its gradient and hessian.

There is however an alternative, the Pseudo Huber Loss, whose formula is:

$$L_\delta(a) = \delta^2 \left( \sqrt{1 + \left(\frac{a}{\delta}\right)^2} - 1 \right)$$

In python this gives :

```python
# ch6_pseudo_huber.py
import math

def pseudo_huber(err):
    delta = 0.99
    loss = delta**2 * (math.sqrt(1 + (err / delta)**2)
        - 1)
    return loss
```

The following plot allows the comparison of this loss function with the absolute error:

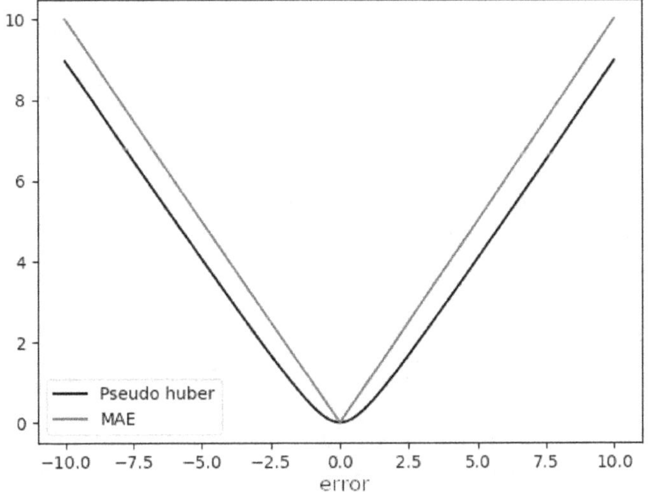


It is therefore a fairly close approximation, which offers the advantage of being regular and of being able to be derived twice, to feed the Gradient Boosting algorithms.

## 7.4  Regularized objectives

This strategy transforming a function that is not derivable into a derivable one is called regularization. The principle is to find a formula that allows one to calculate almost exactly the result of a non-regular function.

The following two functions are an example of what can be done for the absolute error function, which comes up regularly as an objective.

### 7.4.1 Logcosh

As a first step, it is interesting to construct an approximation of the absolute error. The Pseudo Huber Loss seen above is a possibility, but as its plot shows, it deviates a bit from the plot of the absolute error.

To obtain a better approximation, the following formula can be used, based on the combination of the logarithm and cosine hyperbolic:

$$\begin{cases} (1 - \alpha) \cdot log(cosh(x)) & ; & x < 0 \\ \alpha \cdot log(cosh(x)) & ; & x >= 0 \end{cases}$$

Its plot is given by the following curve:

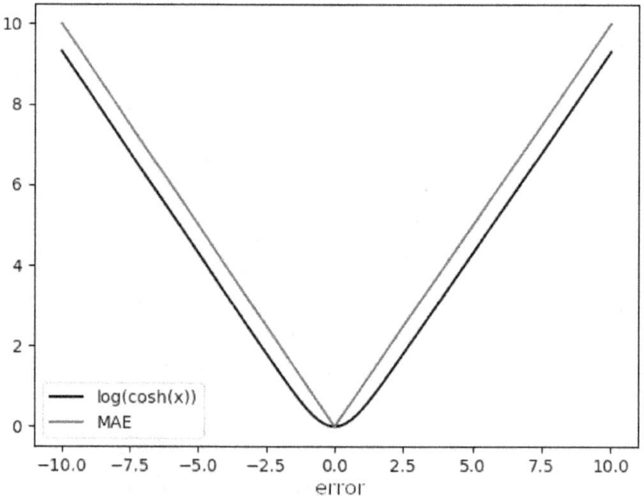


Its implementation in python is trivial:

```python
import math

def logcosh(err):
    loss = math.log(math.cosh(err))
    return loss
```

To understand why this formula gives a good approximation of the absolute error, it is very enlightening to go into the details of the hyperbolic cosine formula:

$$cosh(x) = \frac{e^x + e^{-x}}{2}$$

When x is large enough, the exponential term becomes dominant, and the cosh function can then be approximated by :

$$\frac{e^x}{2}$$

Similarly, when x becomes sufficiently negative, then cosh becomes close to

$$\frac{e^{-x}}{2}$$

Reading these two simplifications, the linear behavior of log(cosh) for sufficiently positive or negative values of x begins to be explained. Indeed, by applying the logarithm function to these approximations, we get for positive x:

$$\begin{aligned} log(cos(x)) &\approx log(\tfrac{e^x}{2}), \forall x, x \gg 0 \\ &\approx log(e^x) - log(2) \\ &\approx x - log(2) \end{aligned}$$

and for x sufficiently negative :

$$\begin{aligned} log(cos(x)) &\approx log(\tfrac{e^{-x}}{2}), \forall x, x \ll 0 \\ &\approx log(e^{-x}) - log(2) \\ &\approx -x - log(2) \end{aligned}$$

In summary, $log(cosh)$ is very close to $x$ for sufficiently large $x$, and $-x$ for sufficiently negative $x$, and this with a constant error of $-log(2)$. It is therefore a good approximation of the absolute value function.

$Log(2)$ is exactly the offset that appears between the absolute error curve and $log(cosh)$.

Since the cosine and the logarithm are derivable, so is the function log(cosh). Its gradient and hessian are calculated as follows:

```python
import numpy as np

def log_cosh(y_true, y_pred):
    err = y_pred - y_true
    grad = np.tanh(err)
    hess = 1 / np.cosh(err)**2
    return grad, hess
```

The next section will show how to use it in XGBoost.

## 7.4.2   Quantile regression

Based on this approximation of the absolute error, it is possible to construct another class of objective function that is very useful for training a model with Gradient Boosting methods: quantile functions.

Before going into the details of these functions, two facts should be remembered: using the squared error as an objective means to predict a mean, while with an approximation of the absolute error, the predictions tend towards the median.

However, it is sometimes interesting not to predict a median, but another quantile, such as the last decile.

To do this, it is possible to modify the $log(cosh)$ function to no longer predict a median, but any quantile. This gives the following formulas:

$$\begin{cases} (1 - \alpha) \cdot log(cosh(x)) & ; \quad x < 0 \\ \alpha \cdot log(cosh(x)) & ; \quad x >= 0 \end{cases}$$

Alpha is used here to specify which quantile is considered. 0.5 is equivalent to using the median, while 0.9 is equivalent to using the last decile.

Graphically, the goal is to have a curve that tends to converge to this type of plot, reproduced for different values of alpha:

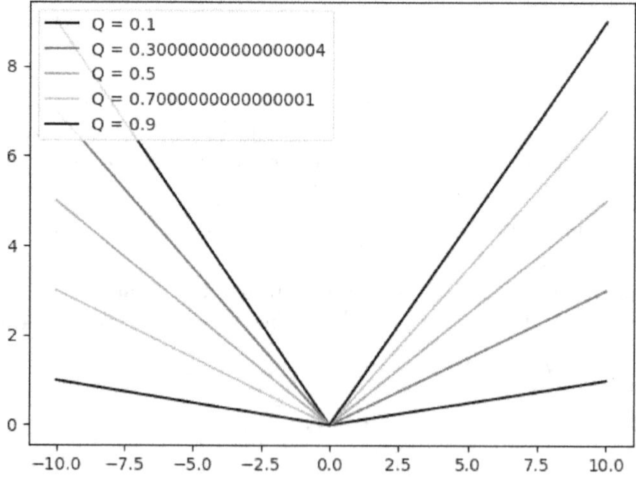


Focusing for example on a value of alpha at 0.2, the above formula provides the following approximation:

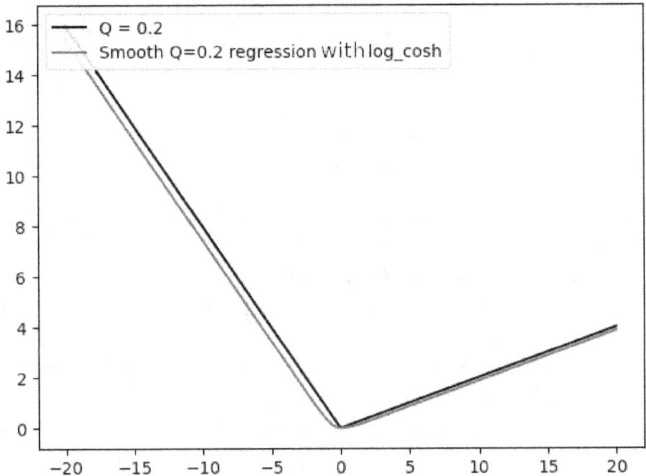


## 7.5  Personalized objectives

As these different functions are not provided by default by the current implementations of Gradient Boosting for decision trees, this section will show how they can be integrated. In particular, the case of XGBoost will be studied in depth.

This section will also show a clever use of quantile functions to predict confidence intervals.

### 7.5.1  XGBoost and quantile regression

The implementation of XGBoost with the scikit-learn interface offers the possibility to define custom objectives. To do so, it is sufficient to pass to the XGBoost model constructor a function taking as input the real and predicted values and producing in return the gradient and the hessian of the considered function. The following lines illustrate this for the quantile function seen above:

```python
import pandas as pd
import numpy as np
from xgboost.sklearn import XGBRegressor
from sklearn.model_selection import ShuffleSplit
import matplotlib.pyplot as plt


# log cosh quantile is a regularized quantile loss
    function
```

```python
def log_cosh_quantile(alpha):
    def _log_cosh_quantile(y_true, y_pred):
        err = y_pred - y_true
        err = np.where(err < 0, alpha * err, (1 - alpha
            ) * err)
        grad = np.tanh(err)
        hess = 1 / np.cosh(err)**2
        return grad, hess
    return _log_cosh_quantile
```

> ☞ Here, to avoid having to write a log_cosh function for
> every possible value of alpha, a higher-level function,
> log_cosh_quantile returns a closure to a function in which
> alpha is captured.

Equipped with this function, we can use it to feed XGBoost, which will use it to calculate the weights of the nodes of the leaves of each tree built. Its use is as simple as the following lines:

```python
clf = XGBRegressor(objective=log_cosh_quantile(1-alpha
    ),
                    n_estimators=125,
                    max_depth=5,
                    n_jobs=6,
                    learning_rate=.05)
```

## 7.5.2   Confidence intervals

As shown in the previous section, quantile functions allow us to predict a quantile instead of the mean or median.

By coupling two predictions, one for a low quantile and the other for a high quantile, it becomes possible to predict confidence intervals.

> ☞ Confidence intervals give instead of a single value an
> interval in which the prediction lies with a probability
> of n %.

The following lines of code illustrate this in the case of predicting the travel time of a taxi. They are based on the Billion Taxi Ride dataset which is retrieved from a local extract:

```python
dateparse = lambda x: pd.datetime.strptime(x, '%Y-%m-%d
    %H:%M:%S')


dtf = pd.read_csv('data/taxi_data.csv',
                parse_dates=['tpep_dropoff_datetime',
                    'tpep_pickup_datetime'],
                date_parser=dateparse)
```

Once the data is loaded, it is pre-processed to extract useful information such as travel time:

```python
dtf['duration'] = (dtf['tpep_dropoff_datetime'] - dtf
    ['tpep_pickup_datetime']).apply(lambda x : x.
    total_seconds() / 60.0)
```

Some cleaning is also done to remove outliers and unnecessary columns:

```python
dtf = dtf[(dtf['duration'] < 90) & (dtf['duration'] >
    0)]

# identify useless columns and drop them
to_drop = ['tpep_dropoff_datetime',
           'tpep_pickup_datetime',
           'store_and_fwd_flag',
           'passenger_count',
           'RatecodeID',
           'store_and_fwd_flag',
           'PULocationID',
           'DOLocationID',
           'payment_type',
           'fare_amount',
           'extra',
           'mta_tax',
           'tip_amount']
dtf.drop(to_drop, axis=1, inplace=True)
```

Then the actual training begins, with a random split between training and test datasets:

```python
splitter = ShuffleSplit(n_splits=1, test_size=.25,
    random_state=0)

alpha = 0.95
to_predict = 'duration'

for train_index, test_index in splitter.split(dtf):
    train = dtf.iloc[train_index]
    test = dtf.iloc[test_index]

    X = train
    y = train[to_predict]
    X.drop([to_predict], axis=1, inplace=True)

    X_test = test
    y_test = test[to_predict]
    X_test.drop([to_predict], axis=1, inplace=True)
```

A first sub-prediction is performed to find the lower bound of the confidence interval:

```
clf = XGBRegressor(objective=log_cosh_quantile(
    alpha),
                        n_estimators=125,
                        max_depth=5,
                        n_jobs=6,
                        learning_rate=.05)

clf.fit(X, y)
y_upper_smooth = clf.predict(X_test)
```

An over-prediction follows this sub-prediction to obtain the upper bound :

```
clf = XGBRegressor(objective=log_cosh_quantile(1-
    alpha),
                        n_estimators=125,
                        max_depth=5,
                        n_jobs=6,
                        learning_rate=.05)

clf.fit(X, y)
y_lower_smooth = clf.predict(X_test)
```

It is then possible to display the actual values and intervals to ensure that they are correct:

```
max_length = 150
fig = plt.figure()
plt.plot(list(y_test[:max_length]), 'gx', label=u'
    Real value')
plt.plot(y_upper_smooth[:max_length], 'y_', label=u
    'Q Superior')
plt.plot(y_lower_smooth[:max_length], 'b_', label=u
    'Q inferior')
index = np.array(range(0, len(y_upper_smooth[:
    max_length])))
plt.fill(np.concatenate([index, index[::-1]]),
        np.concatenate([y_upper_smooth[:max_length
            ], y_lower_smooth[:max_length][::-1]),
        alpha=.5, fc='b', ec='None', label='90%
            confidence interval')
plt.xlabel('$index$')
plt.ylabel('$duration$')
plt.legend(loc='upper left')
plt.show()
```

The following plot is the final proof of the relevance of this approach:

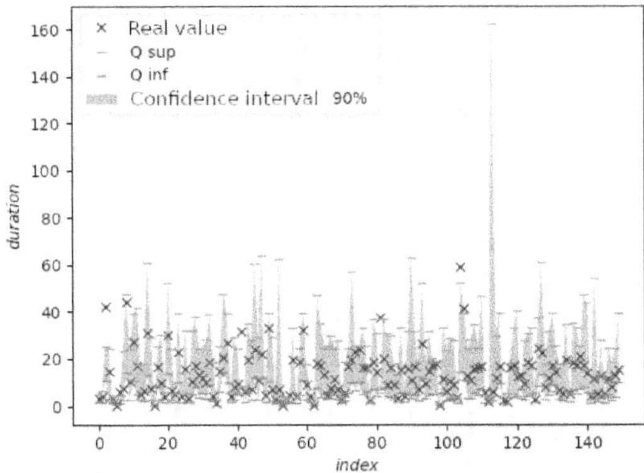

In essence, this confidence interval approach is very attractive. It enriches the predictions with a notion of confidence that allows quantifying the relevance and reliability of a prediction.

# Chapter 8

# Gradient Boosting for time series

## 8.1   Time series

### 8.1.1   Definition

The study and prediction of time series is a well-identified domain of Machine Learning, with its dedicated approaches.

A time series is defined as a set of data, consisting of measurements, called samples, for each of which the precise time at which the measurement was made is known.

This can be for example a simple sound recording, but also an electroencephalogram or a count of the number of customers at the cash register of a store.

The recorded value can be a simple scalar, as in the measurement of a voltage at a specific point in a circuit. It can also be a vector, as in the case of an electroencephalogram where many sensors are involved.

The essential characteristic of time series is therefore this dependence on time, which is specific to evolving systems. These systems are by nature difficult to predict.

The figure below reproduces a time series, where the time is on the abscissa and the sampled value on the ordinate:

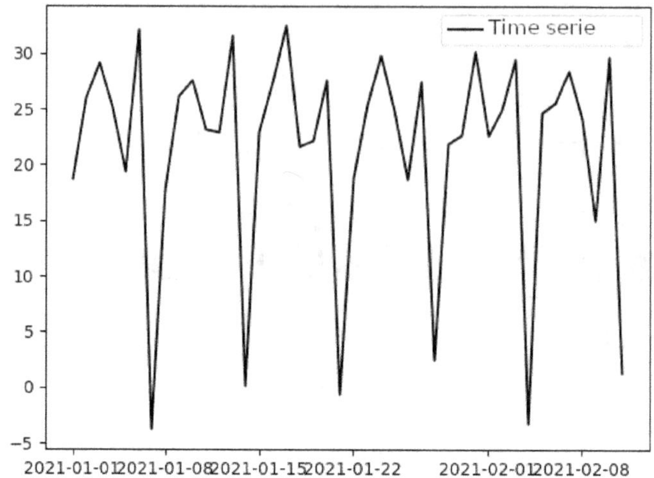


## 8.1.2 Specificities

**Intrinsic**

Two points are responsible for the particular attention that must be paid to the time series.

Firstly, it is this dependence on time, which has been mentioned in introduction. By nature, time is constantly changing, and an instant t in the future is of course not present in the training data.

If it is used as a feature to feed the training of a decision tree, then during the prediction, the time t cannot be linked to any past event.

The second particularity of a time series is the different scales at which it can be considered. For example, it is possible to look at its variations within a second, an hour, a day, a week, a month, ... All these different resolutions carry information, and can contain relevant information for a prediction.

**Processing**

This is not the subject of this book, but time series are subject to particular pre-processing, to make them exploitable.

It can be de-noising, filtering, resampling, oversampling, under-sampling, ...

The whole range of signal processing tools is available to the Data Scientist. One should not hesitate to take advantage of them to provide the model with the most exploitable data possible.

## 8.2 Time series and decision trees

Marrying time series, whose nature is essentially continuous, even if sampling has taken place, with decision tree ensembles, whose structure is discrete requires a good understanding of how the two can be articulated.

This section explores how and with what limitations this coupling can be done.

### 8.2.1 Extrapolation and decision trees

**Limitation**

One point that users of Gradient Boosting methods for decision trees regularly ignore is their total inability to extrapolate.

Indeed, by their very nature and because of the way they are trained, decision trees cannot predict anything other than what they have already encountered during the training phase.

The chapter of this book on the mathematical foundations of Gradient Boosting methods has highlighted that the predictions made by a decision tree only use weighted sums. The weights of the leaves reached after traversing the tree are the only elements involved in the prediction, and their values are linear combinations of the samples of the training dataset.

At no time is one of the input features multiplied by any coefficient to produce the prediction.

Under these conditions, it is completely impossible to extrapolate, i.e. to extend a trend, either downwards or upwards.

A quantity that would have to be predicted, and that would simply double every day, is therefore completely unpredictable by a decision tree.

On the other hand, time series evolve over time, and can often be modeled as a sum of the product between time and functions of the input features of the model.

This divergence of behavior may suggest the inadequacy of tree models for time series, but the following sections will show that this is not always the case.

In the meantime, the following section demonstrates with a few lines of code the inability of decision trees to extrapolate.

### Demonstration

To give substance to these theoretical arguments, the listing below will implement XGBoost to build a predictor for a simple time series that is simply proportional to elapsed time. The results obtained will be used to validate with a plot the ability or not of XGBoost, and of all tree-based models to interpolate and extrapolate.

The code starts by loading the useful modules:

```python
import matplotlib.pyplot as plt
from xgboost import XGBRegressor
import numpy as np
import pandas as pd
```

It then creates an XGBoost model with the default parameters, except for the number of estimators which is increased to 250:

```python
model = XGBRegressor(n_estimators=250)
```

The time series to be learned, lasting 10 seconds, is constructed as being simply proportional to the elapsed time:

```python
ts = np.linspace(0, 10, 100)
X = pd.DataFrame({'ts': ts})

y = ts * 6.66
```

Then it is used to train the predictor :

```python
model.fit(X, y)
```

The latter is finally applied to produce predictions, forcing the use of timestamps shifted by 0.05 to force an interpolation. 5 points outside the training time window are also added, to make sure to extrapolate:

```python
x_preds = pd.DataFrame({'ts': list(ts + 0.05) + [11,
    12, 13, 14, 15]})
preds = model.predict(x_preds)
```

The whole is then displayed :

```python
plt.plot(x_preds, x_preds['ts'] * 6.66, label='Actual
    values')
plt.plot(x_preds, preds, label='Values predicted by
    XGBoost')
plt.legend()

plt.show()
```

The result speaks for itself:

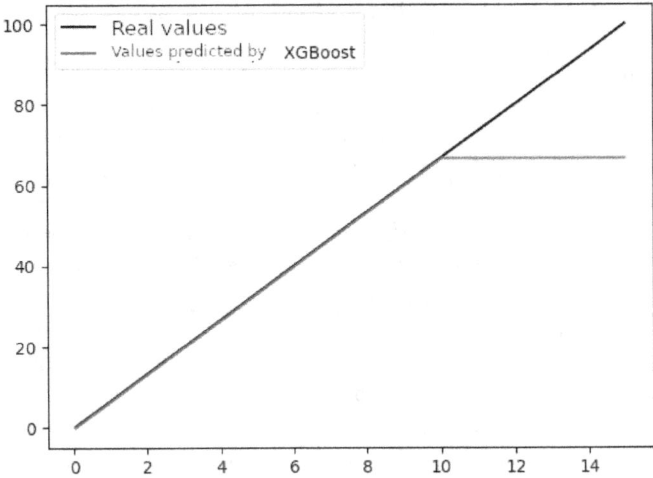


In the 10 seconds range of the training data, the prediction is almost exact, while outside the range the prediction saturates on the last known value of the training.

The constructed decision tree is therefore very accurate inside the known data intervals, but outside this area of knowledge, it simply predicts the closest known value. It, therefore, interpolates very well but fails to extrapolate.

The analysis of the theory proposed above was correct, and it is mathematically impossible for a decision tree to extrapolate, whether as a function of time or anything else. A decision tree can only return what it has learned.

It is crucial to integrate this behavior and to be aware of the possibilities of this type of model.

### Hacking objective functions

Now that we have seen in the chapter on objective functions that they are the core of Gradient Boosting methods, it is legitimate to ask whether it is conceivable to choose a carefully designed objective function that would make extrapolation possible.

Unfortunately, such a hacking of objective functions is not possible. In any case, they are not time-dependent, and nothing in the mathematics deployed to calculate the gains and weights of the sheets involves the time variable.

In this particular context, being able to customize the objective function is unfortunately of no help.

### Alternatives

What are the alternatives that can be implemented to get around this pitfall?

The first is to return to a case where time no longer affects the data. In the language of Data Science, it is a matter of bringing ourselves back to a stationary form, that is to say, one with a structure, potentially complex, but independent of time.

In the example used to show the inability of decision trees to interpolate, it is enough to realize that the series grows linearly, with a slope of 6.66. By predicting not this quantity, but its derivative with respect to time, which is constant, it is possible to return to a case where time no longer intervenes.

Applying one or more derivatives is an expedient regularly used to try to confine oneself to a stationary series.

Making a time series stationary is therefore a first step towards the development of a reliable and accurate decision tree model, but it is not sufficient.

We will then have to discover the underlying structures that govern the behavior of the data studied. And this is precisely a point where Gradient Boosting methods excel.

All that is needed is to provide them with the input data to capture these structures.

## 8.3   Capturing temporal features

Working with a stationary time series does not mean that it does not change with time or that it is constant.

Rather, it means that the series under consideration will not grow or decrease indefinitely. On the other hand, it can be the place of periodic phenomena more or less complex and running at different resolutions.

It can be for example hourly, weekly, monthly, ... and their combination.

### 8.3.1   Simple example of periodicity

The following few lines of code generate a time series representative of a real case. In this case, it is the daily sales of a given product, in a given store:

```python
import matplotlib.pyplot as plt
import numpy as np
import pandas as pd

weekly_sales = [20, 25, 30, 25, 20, 30, 0]
```

```python
X = pd.DataFrame({ 'date': pd.date_range(start='
    1/1/2021', end='30/12/2021'),
                'value': np.array(weekly_sales * 52) +
                    np.random.normal(0, 2, 364)})
```

The series is constructed based on a weekly sales pattern to which a Gaussian noise is added, with a zero mean and a standard deviation of 2.

The series is indeed stationary because the global sales level does not evolve over time.

The resolution of the series is daily, that is to say, each day is associated with a single value. This series extends over 364 days to be a multiple of 7 days.

The plot of this series for the first 7 weeks shows the weekly periodicity, with in particular the zero sales every Sunday:

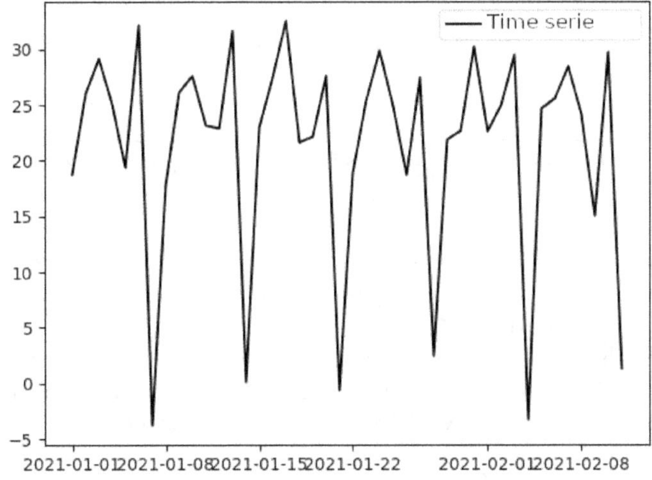


In general, it is interesting when there is a periodic phenomenon as shown in the above plot, to look at the values for recurrent moments of the period. In this case, the period being weekly, it is relevant to look for each day the level of sales.

> ☞ It is important to remember here, as seen in Chapter 4, that when analyzing time series, it is crucial to work with data that are ordered in time. This is especially true when a CrossValidation approach is used. It is therefore necessary to sort them in ascending order according to the time before any manipulation.

This gives the following figure:

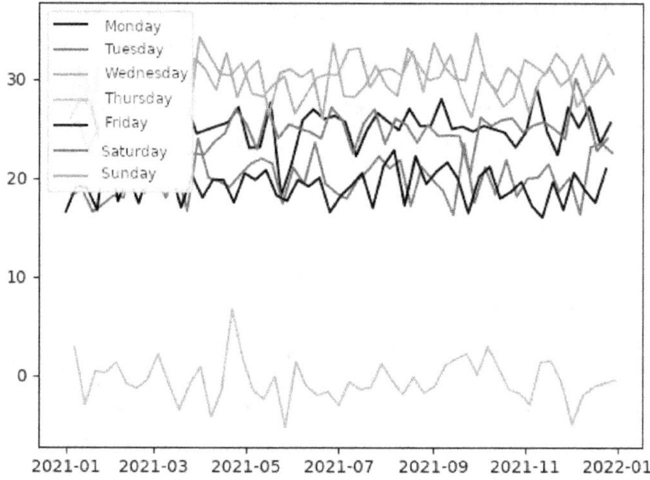


These curves show that when analyzed on a day-of-the-week basis, the variability is much lower than yearly. Predictability is therefore increased.

It is also useful to use a sliding average, once the periodicity has been identified, to convince oneself of the stationary character of the series. A few lines of Python are enough to do this:

```python
import numpy as np
import pandas as pd

weekly_sales = [20, 25, 30, 25, 20, 30, 0]

X = pd.DataFrame({ 'date': pd.date_range(start='1/1/2021', end='30/12/2021'),
                   'value': np.array(weekly_sales * 52) +
                       np.random.normal(0, 2, 364)})

X['smoothed'] = X['value'].ewm(span=7*4).mean()
```

The ewm function takes care of applying a sliding window over the data of this example and applies the mean to it. The span attribute indicates the width of this window, which is taken here to be 4 weeks.

The curve obtained is reproduced in the following figure:

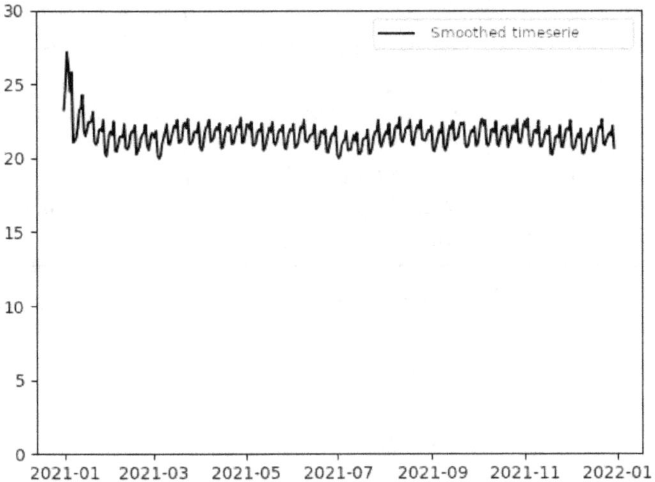

It clearly shows that the series is stationary on this time scale since it is stable. Neither growth nor decay is observed.

## 8.3.2   Manual capture

### Principle

In light of the previous example, it is clear that we will have to enrich the data of the time series. As chapter 3 explained, there are two ways of amending a dataset: exogenous or endogenous.

In the case of time series, the endogenous way is to be preferred. Indeed, there is generally a lot of information in the raw signal that is just waiting to be exploited.

The first way to extract these endogenous data is based on a manual extraction based on a preliminary analysis of the signal.

This involves adding features that will guide the Gradient Boosting methods in the segmentation of the data. These features are generally temporal markers, such as the time of day, the day of the week, the number of the week in the year, and the month. But it can also be the distance to an event, the value at a previous moment, or the average over a period, ...

**Example**

Taking the previous case, the extraction of the day of the week seems for example relevant. Being faced with a case of data sampled daily, and potentially extending over several years, it is also relevant to extract the months but also the weeks attached to each measurement.

> ☞ It is impossible to use time as a feature for a time series. Indeed, as shown in the previous section, decision trees cannot extrapolate. Any time in the future is by definition an unknown value in the model. When making decisions by comparison while traversing the decision trees, the time feature would necessarily always be found in the same leaf. This would always produce the same prediction.

The code below enriches the data from the previous example and builds a LightGBM model on it:

```python
from xgboost import XGBRegressor
import lightgbm as lgb
import matplotlib.pyplot as plt
import numpy as np
import pandas as pd

# Create time serie timestamp indices
monthly_variation = [0.0, 0.0, 0.0, 0.01, 0.05, 0.1,
    0.2, 0.5, 0.4, 0.2, 0.05, 0.0]
weekly_sales = [20, 25, 30, 25, 20, 30, 0]
constant_sales = [10, 10, 10, 10, 10, 10, 10]

X = pd.DataFrame({ 'date': pd.date_range(start='
    01/04/2021', end='01/02/2022'),
                'value': np.array(weekly_sales * 52) +
                    np.random.normal(0, 2, 364)})

X['day_of_week'] = X['date'].apply(lambda date: date.
    day_of_week)
X['month'] = X['date'].apply(lambda date: date.month)

train_data = lgb.Dataset(X[['day_of_week', 'month']],
    label=X['value'])
model = lgb.train({}, train_data)

test = pd.DataFrame({'day_of_week': [0, 1, 2, 3, 4, 5,
    6],
                month': [1, 1, 1, 1, 1, 1, 1]})

pred = model.predict(test)
```

```python
print(pred)
# -> [20.1 25.02 29e.56 24.99 19.47 30.16 1.4e-02]
print(weekly_sales)
# -> [20, 25, 30, 25, 20, 30, 0]
print(pred - np.array(weekly_sales))
# -> [0.12 0.02 -0.43 -0.00 -0.52 0.16 0.01]
```

LightGBM does not have an interface with pandas. It is therefore necessary to transform the training dataset to the internal format of LightGBM: Dataset.

The addition of the month and day of the week features are extracted using date.month and date.day_of_week respectively.

The last three lines validate this approach: the predictions made by LightGBM are very close to the expected values.

LightGBM also offers the possibility to display the importance of each feature. This is what the following lines of code do:

```python
import lightgbm as lgb
import matplotlib.pyplot as plt
import numpy as np
import pandas as pd

weekly_sales = [20, 25, 30, 25, 20, 30, 0]
constant_sales = [10, 10, 10, 10, 10, 10, 10]

X = pd.DataFrame({ 'date': pd.date_range(start='
    01/04/2021', end='01/02/2022'),
                  'value': np.array(weekly_sales * 52) +
                      np.random.normal(0, 2, 364)})

X['day_of_week'] = X['date'].apply(lambda date: date.
    day_of_week)
X['month'] = X['date'].apply(lambda date: date.month)

train_data = lgb.Dataset(X[['day_of_week', 'month']],
    label=X['value'])
model = lgb.train({}, train_data)

lgb.plot_importance(model, importance_type='gain')
plt.show()
```

This allows for highlighting the weight of the constructed features in the prediction. The obtained graph is in agreement with what the various previous plots suggested, namely that it is indeed the day of the week that explains the level of sales.

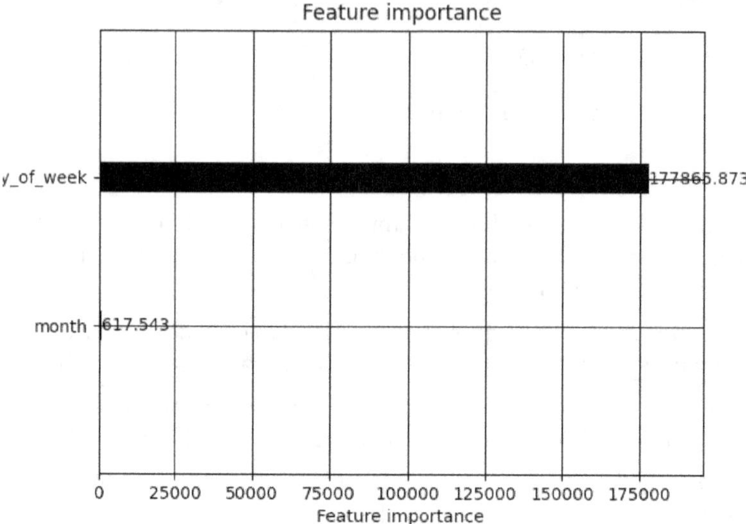


## Bestiary of computable features

Features of different natures can be generated to enrich the time series.

In essence, the computable features can be grouped into the following classes:

- Temporal markers: time of day, week, month, ... they are used to identify a period, a recurrence in the data. They bring up the rhythm of the series.

- Temporal characteristics: these are indicators that allow us to classify time series according to their behavior. The coefficients of a Fourier transform or a wavelet decomposition are examples. It is also possible to perform auto-correlation of the series considered with itself to show seasonality.

- Trend indicators: even if, as shown at the beginning of this chapter, decision trees cannot extrapolate, it is still possible to account for an increasing or decreasing trend in a prediction based on measurements at specific moments in the past. It can be for example the value at D-1, D-2, D-3, ...

The following code illustrates this concept on a simple model inspired by meteorology. Indeed, in meteorology, any model must at least beat the following predictor: tomorrow's weather is essentially the same as today's. Applied to temperature, this gives:

```python
import numpy as np
import pandas as pd
from xgboost import XGBRegressor

temperature = pd.DataFrame({ 'date': pd.date_range(
    start='01/04/2021', end='01/02/2022'),
                        temperature': np.random.
                            normal(14, 5, 364)})

temperature['temperature_D-1'] = temperature['
    temperature'].shift(1)

model = XGBRegressor(n_estimators=1250, max_depth=5)

model.fit(temperature[['temperature_J-1']], temperature
    ['temperature'])

pred = model.predict(pd.DataFrame({'temperature_D-1' :
    [17, 18, 19]}))

print(pred)
# -> [20.2686 15.555077 14.99681 ]
```

The trend indicator here is the temperature of the previous day,
calculated using the shift function, which simply shifts the time
series by one day.

### 8.3.3 Automatic extraction

Some of the features mentioned in the previous paragraphs can
be calculated automatically and in a very exhaustive way. This
is for example what the tsfresh library allows, which can extract
hundreds of features from a time series.

Tsfresh extracts a large variety of different features, starting
with statistical metrics such as the mean, the minimum, the maximum, the variance, the number of sign changes, ... but also simple
characteristics of the signal, such as the amplitude, the spectrum,
the Fourier transform coefficients, the energy, the entropy, and all
kinds of correlation. The enrichment of the time series is then very
complete.

These features can then be used for classification as well as for
regression. Gradient Boosting methods will identify which of these
features are relevant. The features that do not contribute anything
will be discarded when selecting the decision criteria that bring the
most gain.

### Application to a simple case

Since code is worth a thousand words, the example of sales-level prediction will be used here to illustrate the use of automatic generators of temporal features. The tsfresh library, the most advanced in this domain, will be used here.

To do so, the following case study is used: for two products, one characterized by a weekly sales pattern, and the other purely constant, the daily sales level must be predicted.

The above code starts by building the two-time series, for each of these two products:

```python
from tsfresh import extract_features
from tsfresh.feature_extraction.settings import
    MinimalFCParameters
import lightgbm as lgb
import matplotlib.pyplot as plt
import numpy as np
import pandas as pd

# Create time serie timestamp indices
monthly_variation = [0.0, 0.0, 0.0, 0.01, 0.05, 0.1,
    0.2, 0.5, 0.4, 0.2, 0.05, 0.0]
weekly_sales = [20, 25, 30, 25, 20, 30, 0]
constant_sales = [10, 10, 10, 10, 10, 10, 10]


product_0 = pd.DataFrame({ 'date': pd.date_range(start=
    '01/04/2021', end='01/02/2022'),
                'value': np.array(weekly_sales * 52) +
                    np.random.normal(0, 2, 364),
                'product_id': [0] * 364})
product_1 = pd.DataFrame({ 'date': pd.date_range(start=
    '01/04/2021', end='01/02/2022'),
                'value': np.array(constant_sales * 52)
                    + np.random.normal(0, 2, 364),
                'product_id': [1] * 364})
```

Product 0 follows a weekly sales pattern, with zero sales on Sunday. Product 1, on the other hand, sells consistently throughout the week, including Sunday.

```python
product_2 = pd.DataFrame({ 'date': pd.date_range(start=
    '01/04/2021', end='01/02/2022'),
                'value': np.array(weekly_sales * 52) +
                    np.random.normal(0, 2, 364),
                'product_id': [2] * 364})
product_3 = pd.DataFrame({ 'date': pd.date_range(start=
    '01/04/2021', end='01/02/2022'),
                'value': np.array(constant_sales * 52)
                    + np.random.normal(0, 2, 364),
```

```
                    'product_id': [3] * 364})
```

Products 2 and 3 are built on the same model and will be used to
test the prediction. Product 2 sees its sales vary during the week,
while for product 3 the sales are stable. The training dataset is
built by concatenating the time series of products 0 and 1:

```
X = pd.concat([product_0, product_1])
```

The test dataset, for its part, aggregates the data of products
2 and 3:

```
test = pd.concat([product_2, product_3])
From these time series will be automatically extracted
    a set of features using tsfresh, through the
    extract_features method:


features = extract_features(timeseries_container=X,
                    column_id="product_id",
                        column_value='value',
                        column_sort="date",
                    default_fc_parameters=
                        MinimalFCParameters())
```

For this example, only a minimal set of features is extracted, so as
not to generate too many and to limit the computation time.

Indeed, tsfresh can extract hundreds of indicators, and this for
each time series. This can quickly become expensive in terms of
computation time. This restriction is done by passing the Mini-
malFCParameters parameter during the extraction.

> ☞ Other options are possible to control the feature gener-
> ation. For example, there is an efficient configuration
> that groups the most relevant ones. It is also possible
> to calculate all of them. This mode is to be reserved
> for an exploration phase. Note that it is also possible
> to select the features one by one.

The key identifying each time series is given by the column_id
parameter. This is the product_id column, which contains a unique
identifier for each product. The features will be extracted for each
of the two products.

The dataset containing the extracted features is then reinte-
grated in the initial pandas dataframe, by joining on the product
ids:

```
features = features.rename_axis('product_id').
    reset_index()
X = X.merge(features, on=['product_id'])
```

Finally, the series is enriched with the day of the week:

```python
X['day_of_week'] = X['date'].apply(lambda date: date.
    day_of_week)
```

The same pre-processing is applied to the test dataset:

```python
features = extract_features(timeseries_container=test,
                        column_id="product_id",
                        column_value='value',
                        column_sort="date",
                        default_fc_parameters=
                        MinimalFCParameters())

features = features.rename_axis('product_id').
    reset_index()
test = test.merge(features, on=['product_id'])
test['day_of_week'] = test['date'].apply(lambda date:
    date.day_of_week)
```

A training function of a few lines is then added, to quickly test the relevance of the addition of automatically generated features on the quality of the prediction:

```python
model = None
def train_and_predict(flist, test_set):
    train_data = lgb.Dataset(X[flist], label=X['value'
        ])
    model = lgb.train({}, train_data)
    pred = model.predict(test_set[flist])
    return pred
The latter is applied to the prediction of product 2,
    whose sales vary within the week:
features_list = features.columns.to_list() + ['
    day_of_week']
pred = train_and_predict(features_list, test[test['
    product_id'] == 2])
print(pred[:7])
# -> [20.43 25.08 30.39 24.61 20.04 30.14 -0.19]
print(weekly_sales)
# -> [20, 25, 30, 25, 20, 30, 0]
```

The results are close to those expected. The model captured the variability well thanks to the day_of_week feature. The features of tsfresh allowed us to make the distinguo between the two sales modes. Applied to the second product, the model also produces good results:

```python
pred = train_and_predict(features_list, test[test['
    product_id'] == 3])

print(pred[:7])
# -> [10.17 9.75 10.06 9.95 9.94 10.14 10.28]
```

```
print(constant_sales)
# -> [10, 10, 10, 10, 10, 10, 10]
```

If on the other hand the tsfresh features are not incorporated in the model, and only day_of_week is used, then the model is no longer able to distinguish the two sales modes. It then predicts the same thing for both products:

```
pred = train_and_predict(['day_of_week'], test[test['
    product_id'] == 2])
print(pred[:7])
# -> [14.90 17.50 20.01 17.38 15.07 20.18 5.27]
print(weekly_sales)

pred = train_and_predict(['day_of_week'], test[test['
    product_id'] == 3])

print(pred[:7])
# -> [14.90 17.50 20.01 17.38 15.07 20.18 5.27]
print(constant_sales)
# -> [10, 10, 10, 10, 10, 10, 10]
```

This example is particularly minimal, but it clearly shows the benefit of automatically adding temporal features. The care of their construction is not left to the data scientist, which is an obvious time saver but also allows for greater completeness.

The downside is the computation time, which can become prohibitive for deep histories and a large number of unique time series.

**Particularities of temporal features**

It is essential to understand that the features extracted from a time series do not characterize the collected samples, but the time series itself.

They, therefore, do not help in the prediction directly but are a needle in the segmentation of the different behaviors in time.

## 8.3.4  Multi-model approach

It may be interesting to combine automatic feature generation with dimension reduction and clustering.

This allows to group time series with similar behaviors in the same cluster.

It can then be interesting to treat these different clusters individually, by training a specific model for each one.

The last chapter of this book will discuss in detail the possibilities of a multi-model approach.

## 8.4  Construction of training and test datasets

To conclude this chapter, it is important to insist on the fact that one must be extremely careful when building training and test datasets.

### 8.4.1  Partitioning

In particular, care must be taken to ensure that the construction of the training and validation/test datasets used in the Cross Validation phases is perfectly hermetic.

Indeed, it is imperative to build all the features independently on these two types of datasets. In no case should you add temporal features before doing the splitting.

On the contrary, you must first split the data into training and test datasets, and then enrich the two types of datasets.

### 8.4.2  Data leakage

If this partitioning was not scrupulously respected, the model would be faced with a data leakage problem during the training phase. That is to say that the test datasets, located in the future, would have features calculated in part with data from the future.

There would then be a bias in the model that would lead to overfitting. The performances would be excellent during training, but would not generalize during prediction in real conditions.

### 8.4.3  Respect of the temporality

It is also necessary to make sure that the test datasets are in the future compared to the training datasets. The splitting to constitute the datasets for the cross-validation must be done with functions dedicated to this use, such as TimeSerieSplit of scikit learn. Methods such as Kfold would not be relevant.

# Chapter 9

# XGBoost, LightGBM, or Catboost, which library to choose?

## 9.1 Why choose ?

### 9.1.1 Motivations

There are in the open source world three main libraries to train decision trees by applying the Gradient Boosting method.

All three are very efficient, both in terms of the accuracy obtained by the generated models and the training time.

However, despite their common excellence, they are not equivalent and all have their advantages and disadvantages on specific points.

This chapter will take an in-depth look at each of the differences between these three designs. This comparative analysis will be done through the prism of the different answers brought by each of them to the main questions that arise when implementing a Gradient Boosting approach.

### 9.1.2 From theory to practice

The chapter on the mathematical foundations of Gradient Boosting methods for training decision trees has exposed the main theoretical principles.

XGBoost, LightGBM, and CatBoost differ from each other in the ways they move from theory to practice.

The following subsections present the points where there is room for different technical solutions and where each library competes in creativity.

The following paragraphs present the different theoretical points where several technical solutions are possible.

## Selection of the feature and the decision criterion

The first question that a code implementing a Gradient Boosting method for decision trees must face is the choice of the feature to retain for a node and of the value partitioning the data into two subsets.

Indeed, it is the very essence of Gradient Boosting methods to provide a precise mathematical framework to identify this feature/decision threshold pair.

The compromise to be made here is motivated by the need to be exhaustive and to consider all the possibilities, on one hand, and the need to keep computation times within acceptable limits, on the other.

Each library, therefore, places the cursor between these two needs at a different level.

## Support of categorical features

The basic postulate to be satisfied to use a decision tree is that it is possible to order the values associated with a feature. This makes it possible to partition the samples of the training dataset according to this feature.

The problem is that the features characterizing a data sample are not always numbers. They are then categorical features, which are generally represented by strings of characters. This can be for example a color: red, green, blue or a country: France, Germany, or Belgium.

It is not possible to compare them directly unless you use the lexicographical order, which would not necessarily be relevant.

Each of the libraries presented here has its conviction on the subject and proposes a technical solution accordingly.

## Parallelization and distribution

As the volumes of data available to data scientists are increasingly large, the calculation times increase proportionally.

It is therefore essential to be able to distribute or at least parallelize the calculations to guarantee acceptable execution times.

The question of the support of GPU-type co-processors is also to be considered, their use being able to significantly boost the calculation times.

Here again, there is no good answer. XGBoost, LightGBM, and CatBoost each have their specificities.

## Hyper Parameters

The chapter on fine-tuning hyperparameters returned to the importance of choosing the right parameters to govern the construction and configuration of decision tree sets.

Even if there is a set of common parameters that can be found in each of the implementations, the fact remains that the three libraries each expose additional parameters.

Depending on the targeted problem, having control over this or that parameter can be a crucial advantage with a major impact on performance.

A gain in accuracy but also in computation time can result from this.

## Choice and customization of the objective function

The entire construction of the decision trees is based on the objective function. As a reminder, it is the objective function that controls the choice of features and the decision criterion for each node.

Having a large choice of objective functions, or even better, the possibility of adding them manually is an undeniable advantage.

Having and mastering those three different libraries is an asset.

## Interfacing

The generation of a Machine Learning model is only one part of an application. It is necessary to be able to interface this model with other libraries of the Python ecosystem, both upstream to feed it, and downstream to analyze and exploit the results but also to predict.

In this respect, XGBoost, LightGBM, and CatBoost are variously endowed.

## Simplicity of use

Getting to grips with a library can sometimes prove to be a complicated task. In the case of machine learning, this is even more true.

Many parameters must be set, data must undergo a series of treatments to be ingested for training a model. Interpreting the results and validating them is not an easy task.

In this respect, each of the three implementations offers a different approach, the ease of use varying from one to another according to the use cases.

### Implementation language

Still related to performance, it is interesting to ask the question of the language used to implement the core of these methods.

Even if they are often used through the Python language, the critical parts of the implementation are often done in a lower-level language.

A specific need at this level may lead to a specific library.

### Support for missing values

Last point, which is not essential but is very useful: the support of missing values. It is frequent, even inevitable, to be confronted with data sets for which certain columns are not filled in for certain rows.

Dealing with these absences implies arbitrating between getting rid of incomplete rows, by depriving oneself of a part of the data, or conversely keeping them by filling the gaps with substitutes, at the risk of introducing a bias.

Some implementations propose to deal natively with the problem, which is an advantage to consider, provided that one understands what is done with these missing values.

### 9.1.3   Convictions

The following sections detail the convictions and technological choices made by the teams developing XGBoost, LightGBM, and Cat-Boost.

## 9.2   XGBoost

First things first. This comparison between XGBoost, LightGBM, and CatBoost opens with XGBoost. It is the best-known library that takes advantage of Gradient Boosting methods to train sets of decision trees.

At the time of writing, XGBoost had no less than 22,000 stars on Github, the open-source code-sharing platform. This is a very good indicator of the value of a library.

This figure is to be compared to those obtained by LightGBM and CatBoost, which are respectively 13 000 and 6 000 stars.

In the same vein, and this was mentioned in the introduction to this book, XGBoost is the top algorithm that wins the Kaggle Data Science platform tests, in the category of problems with structured data.

The reasons for this success lie in the options XGBoost has taken to implement Gradient Boosting.

## 9.2.1 Choices made

### Feature and decision criterion selection

In the fifth chapter of this work, in the section devoted to the SHAP method and the calculation of Shapley values, the code used to train a set of decision trees uses the technique used by XGBoost.

The approach used to select the most relevant feature and decision threshold is to exhaustively explore all possibilities.

To do so, for each feature, the data samples of the training dataset are sorted in ascending order, according to the feature. The gain is then systematically evaluated for each of the possible separation thresholds.

The threshold with the highest gain for a feature is retained as the best, and the feature with the highest gain is retained as the best.

This method implies a sorting for each feature, and a calculation of the gain for each separation criterion. As a consequence, it is a computationally intensive approach, and it is only applicable to datasets of reasonable size.

To overcome this limitation in terms of computation time, XG-Boost offers 4 modes of gain computation, and thus of feature selection:

- The exact mode, which implements the solution just described

- Two modes based on an original approach detailed in the seminal paper of XGBoost

- A mode inspired by the method implemented in LightGBM and on which we will come back in the section dedicated to LightGBM.

The small script below shows the impact in terms of computation time of each of these 4 variants, first as a function of the number of lines, then as a function of the number of features:

```python
# ch8_feature_selection.py
from xgboost import XGBRegressor
from sklearn.datasets import make_regression
import matplotlib.pyplot as plt
import time

nb_samples = [100, 1000, 2000, 4000, 6000, 8000,
              10000, 20000, 40000, 60000, 80000, 100000]
```

```python
nb_features = [10, 20, 30, 40, 50, 75, 80, 100, 200,
    500]

def train(method):
    elapsed = []
    for n_samples in nb_samples:
        x_train, y_train = make_regression(n_samples=
            n_samples,
                                            n_features=20,
                                            noise=1,
                                            random_state=42)
        model = XGBRegressor(tree_method=method)
        t = time.process_time()
        model.fit(x_train, y_train)
        elapsed_time = time.process_time() - t
        elapsed.append(elapsed_time)
        print('Model trained in ', elapsed_time, 's
            with', method)
    return elapsed
```

This first function measures the computation time for a given method and datasets of various sizes.

```python
def train_features(method):
    elapsed = []
    for n_features in nb_features:
        x_train, y_train = make_regression(n_samples
            =10000,
                                            n_features=
                                                n_features,
                                            noise=1,
                                            random_state=42)
        model = XGBRegressor(tree_method=method)
        t = time.process_time()
        model.fit(x_train, y_train)
        elapsed_time = time.process_time() - t
        elapsed.append(elapsed_time)
        print('Model trained in ', elapsed_time, 's
            with', method)
    return elapsed
```

This second one follows the same principle but varies the number of features. The rest of the code calls these functions for the different calculation modes offered by XGBoost, then plots the results:

```python
exact_time = train('exact')
approx_time = train('approx')
hist_time = train('hist')

plt.style.use('grayscale')
plt.plot(nb_samples, exact_time, label='Exact method')
```

```python
plt.plot(nb_samples, approx_time, label='Approx method'
    )
plt.plot(nb_samples, hist_time, label='Hist method')

plt.xlabel('Number of rows')
plt.ylabel('Calculation time')

plt.legend(loc='upper left')
plt.savefig('xgb_fs.png')
plt.show()

exact_time = train_features('exact')
approx_time = train_features('approx')
hist_time = train_features('hist')

plt.style.use('grayscale')
plt.plot(nb_samples, exact_time, label='Exact method')
plt.plot(nb_samples, approx_time, label='Approx method'
    )
plt.plot(nb_samples, hist_time, label='Hist method')

plt.xlabel('Number of rows')
plt.ylabel('Calculation time')

plt.legend(loc='upper left')
plt.savefig('xgb_fs_feature.png')
plt.show()
```

The calculation time as a function of the number of rows evolves as follows, depending on how the decision thresholds are calculated:

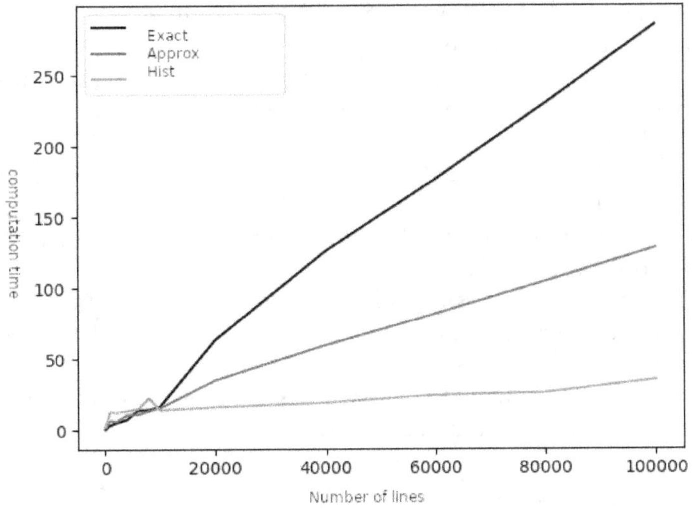

The method inspired by LightGBM is the least impacted by the number of features. The two others see their computation time growing linearly with the number of lines. This is the expected behavior given the method which is essentially proportional to the number of lines, once the sorting is done.

The behavior is essentially the same when the number of features to explore varies:

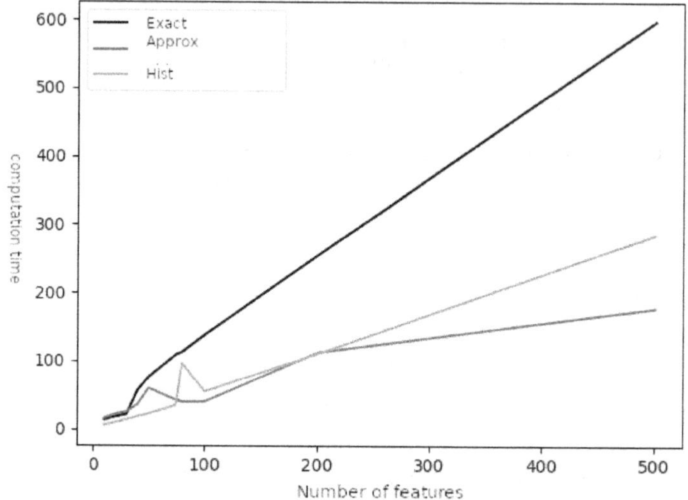


## Support of categorical features

This is one of the weaknesses of XGBoost: it does not natively support categorical features.

As explained in the chapter on training first models, it is necessary to apply some pre-processing on such features, to feed XGBoost with them.

Several options are available. The most commonly implemented is the application of one-hot encoding. This is an operation that transforms a column with n different categories into n columns with simply two values 0 or 1.

The downside of this simplicity is that the number of columns in the dataset increases in proportion to the number of different categories.

Several libraries allow doing one hot encoding. The most commonly used is the get_dummies function of pandas:

```
# ch8_xgb_one_hot_encoding.py
import pandas as pd
```

```
# With pandas
serie = pd.Series(['Category 1', 'Category 2', '
    Category 1', 'Category 3', 'Category 1'])
print(pd.get_dummies(serie))
# -> Category 1 Category 2 Category 3
# -> 0 1 0 0
# -> 1 0 1 0
# -> 2 1 0 0
# -> 3 0 0 1
# -> 4 1 0 0
```

In this example, each row containing a category has been replaced by three columns. A 1 in the column indicates that the corresponding column was present while 0 points to its absence.

Among the possible alternatives to one hot encoding, the chapter detailing the construction of the first models presents GLMM encoding and target encoding.

## Parallelization and distribution

XGBoost has been designed to be easily distributed within a computing cluster.

Several backends are available, the simplest to implement is probably the one based on Kubernetes.

This is the most richly endowed library on this topic.

## Hyper Parameters

XGBoost exposes a large number of hyperparameters. In addition to those already explained in the chapter on Hyper Parameters, the following are interesting:

- booster: this parameter expands the scope of XGBoost, allowing not only gradient boosting methods to be used for decision trees, but also using a simple linear function as the underlying structure. Even more promising, it is possible to use Dart as an underlying model, which allows us to bring the Dropout techniques of Deep Learning to the Gradient Boosting method.

- tree_method, which has just been seen and drives the choice of the best feature.

## Choice and customization of the objective feature

XGBoost not only allows one to choose among many objectives but also offers extreme flexibility by allowing one to implement any objective feature.

As explained at length in the chapter on the proper use of objective functions, having total control over these functions allows for very profitable customization of the generated models.

### Interfacing

Here again, XGBoost stands out, as it can be used from the following languages: Python, R, Java, Julia, Ruby, C, C++, and Swift.

> ☞ It is important to note that it is possible to train a model in one language and use it for prediction in another.

### Simplicity of use

XGBoost is not necessarily the easiest to learn, especially because of the lack of support for categorical features.

This requires pre-processing of the data, which is not excessively complicated but slows down the learning curve.

On the other hand, the native support for missing values balances this limitation.

### Implementation language

XGBoost is implemented in C. This guarantees a level of performance as close as possible to the potential of a CPU.

The part allowing to deport the calculations on GPU is done with Cuda.

### Support for missing values

XGBoost natively supports missing values. To do this, it identifies, at training time, which path maximizes the gain. This is what it calls the default path.

In the absence of data for the considered feature, this path is used.

## 9.2.2   Example

To illustrate the implementation of XGBoost in a case study, the following listing uses data from the Adult dataset, collected by the UCI university. This dataset gathers social and economic data from a cohort of individuals.

The goal is to establish a classification that determines if the individual's salary level will exceed 50,000 dollars.

The following listing shows how to perform such a classification with XGBoost. This is one of the most complicated codes in this chapter because XGBoost does not natively support categorical features. A pre-processing is, therefore, necessary to feed XGBoost:

```python
# ch8_xgboost_example.py
from xgboost import XGBClassifier
from sklearn.model_selection import train_test_split
from sklearn.metrics import classification_report,
    confusion_matrix, accuracy_score
import numpy as np
import pandas as pd

train = pd.read_csv('data/adult.csv')
test = pd.read_csv('data/adult_test.csv')

features = ['age', 'workclass', 'fnlwgt', 'education',
    'education-num',
        'marital-status', 'occupation', 'relationship',
            'sex', 'capital-gain',
            'capital-loss', 'hour-per_week', 'native-
                country', 'income']
to_predict = 'income

categorical_features_indices = np.where(train.dtypes !=
    'int64')[0]
categorical_features = list(train.columns[np.where(
    train.dtypes != np.int64)[0]])

one_hot_cols = []
for col in categorical_features:
    s = train[col].unique()

    one_hot_df = pd.get_dummies(s, prefix='%s_' % col)
    one_hot_df[col] = s

    train = train.merge(one_hot_df, on=[col], how="left
        ")

    one_hot_cols += list(set(one_hot_df.columns.tolist
        ()) - set([col]))

    s = test[col].unique()

    one_hot_df = pd.get_dummies(s, prefix='%s_' % col)
    one_hot_df[col] = s

    test = test.merge(one_hot_df, on=[col], how="left")

X = train[one_hot_cols]
y = train[to_predict]
```

The following category is not present in the test dataset while
it exists in the training dataset. It should be added:

```python
test['native-country__ Holand-Netherlands'] = 0

X_test = test[one_hot_cols]
y_test = test[to_predict]

X.rename(columns={'income__ >50K': 'income__ GT 50K',
                  'income__ <=50K': 'income__ LT 50K'},
         inplace=True)
X_train, X_validation, y_train, y_validation =
    train_test_split(X, y, train_size=0.7, random_state
    =42)

model = XGBClassifier()
model.fit(X_train, y_train, eval_set=[(X_validation,
    y_validation)])


pred = model.predict(X_test)
print(classification_report(test[to_predict], pred))
# Name:  income, Length:  16281, dtype:  object
# precision recall f1-score support
#
# <=50K 1.00 1.00 1.00 12435
# >50K 1.00 1.00 1.00 3846
#
# accuracy 1.00 16281
# macro avg 1.00 1.00 1.00 16281
# weighted avg 1.00 1.00 1.00 16281
print(confusion_matrix(test[to_predict], pred))
# [[12435 0]
# [ 0 3846]]
print(accuracy_score(test[to_predict], pred))
# 1.0
```

The classification performs very well, as shown by the different
scores above and the confusion matrix.


## 9.3   LightGBM

### 9.3.1   Biases

**Feature and decision criterion selection**

LightGBM differs from XGBoost in the way the decision thresholds
are calculated, even if in the previous section it was detailed that
it is possible to use a similar method.

Unlike the default way of working of XGBoost, LightGBM simplifies the task, by not evaluating the gains associated with all possible decision thresholds for a feature.

Instead, it builds a histogram of n bins in which the samples attached to a node are distributed. The algorithm then evaluates only as many decision thresholds as there are bins.

The maximum number of bins is controlled by the hyperparameter max_bin and is 255 by default.

This number is to be compared to the tens or hundreds of thousands of rows that can be found in a training dataset, and for which the exact method of XGBoost will evaluate the gain associated with the related threshold.

The gain in computation time is therefore considerable, even if it must be remembered that it comes at the expense of accuracy.

Another option offered by LightGBM is the GOSS method, which works on a subsample of the data. These are the ones for which the gradient is the highest.

## Support for categorical features

Unlike XGBoost, LightGBM natively supports categorical features.

To do so, it uses an alternative to one hot encoding: integer encoding. The principle of this method is simply to arbitrarily associate an integer with a category.

The type of the feature changes from a string to an integer, and it becomes possible to make comparisons, and thus to feed a decision node.

To overcome the arbitrariness of category numbering, LightGBM uses Fisher's method which optimally partitions the samples into two groups for the categorical feature considered.

The major advantage compared to one hot encoding is that no additional columns are added. This avoids having to build too deep trees and limits the risk of building unbalanced datasets.

## Parallelization and distribution

Parallelizing the training of a decision tree when the Gradient Boosting method is implemented is done quite naturally by distributing the work to each feature.

Indeed, each worker can calculate for a given feature which decision threshold will bring the maximum gain.

Once the calculations are done by each worker, they are pooled, and the feature bringing the maximum gain is retained.

LightGBM follows this approach for parallelization with the particularity of transmitting all the data to all the workers, to minimize the exchanges.

Note also that LightGBM can benefit from the presence of GPUs to accelerate calculations.

At the time of writing, the frameworks accepted for distributing calculations were Dask and Apache Spark, which makes it less versatile than XGBoost.

## Hyper Parameters

A unique option offered by LightGBM in its hyperparameters is the support of linear instead of constant predictors for the weights assigned to the leaves of the decision trees.

When this mode is used, by setting the linear_tree option to True, the value of each leaf is proportional to the value of the features attached to that leaf.

## Choosing and customizing the objective function

Like XGBoost, LightGBM allows the use of a homemade objective function to tailor the Gradient Boosting method to particular needs.

The accepted format is the same as for XGBoost: a function taking input predictions and real values and returning the gradient and the Hessian.

## Interfacing

LightGBM is a little less richly endowed than XGBoost in terms of supported languages. However, it supports the most common ones in Data Science, namely R and Python, and can also interface with C, its implementation language.

## Simplicity of use

LightGBM is relatively easy to use, thanks in part to the native support of categorical features.

The necessity to use the internal data format of LightGBM is however a bit confusing and implies having to transform data that would have been manipulated using pandas.

## Implementation language

LightGBM is implemented in C, as it is usually the case when performance is critical.

**Support for missing values**

Like XGBoost, LightGBM supports incomplete data and thus the presence of missing data.

## 9.3.2 Example

The same example as the one used for XGBoost is reused here. The major change is the absence of one hot encoding since LightGBM takes care of the categorical data processing:

```python
# ch8_lgbm_example.py
from lightgbm import LGBMClassifier
from sklearn.model_selection import train_test_split
from sklearn.metrics import classification_report,
    confusion_matrix, accuracy_score
import numpy as np
import pandas as pd

train = pd.read_csv('data/adult.csv')
test = pd.read_csv('data/adult_test.csv')

features = ['age', 'workclass', 'fnlwgt', 'education',
    'education-num',
        'marital-status', 'occupation', 'relationship',
            'sex', 'capital-gain',
                'capital-loss', 'hour-per_week', 'native-
                    country', 'income']
to_predict = 'income'

X = train[features]
y = train[to_predict]

X_train, X_validation, y_train, y_validation =
    train_test_split(X, y,train_size=0.7, random_state
    =42)

categorical_features_indices = np.where(train.dtypes !=
    'int64')[0]
categorical_features = list(train.columns[np.where(
    train.dtypes != np.int64)[0]])
```

Small specificity of LightGBM, it is necessary to assign the type categorical data to category, otherwise, it fails to process them:

```python
for feature in categorical_features:
    X_train[feature] = pd.Series(X_train[feature],
        dtype="category")
    X_validation[feature] = pd.Series(X_validation[
        feature], dtype="category")
    test[feature] = pd.Series(test[feature], dtype="
        category")
```

```
model = LGBMClassifier()
model.fit(X_train, y_train, eval_set=(X_validation,
    y_validation),
          categorical_feature=categorical_features)

pred = model.predict(test[features])
print(classification_report(test[to_predict], pred))
# Name:  income, Length:  16281, dtype:  object
# precision recall f1-score support
#
# <=50K 1.00 1.00 1.00 12435
# >50K 1.00 1.00 1.00 3846
#
# accuracy 1.00 16281
# macro avg 1.00 1.00 1.00 16281
# weighted avg 1.00 1.00 1.00 16281
print(confusion_matrix(test[to_predict], pred))
# [[12435 0]
# [ 0 3846]]
print(accuracy_score(test[to_predict], pred))
# 1.0
```

The whole code is very similar to XGBoost. This interchange-ability is interesting because it allows us to switch easily from one implementation to another at a low cost.

The results obtained here are very good. The algorithm never makes misclassifications.

## 9.4   CatBoost

CatBoost is the challenger of the three libraries presented here. Less used than the first two, it benefits from features that make it relevant in certain situations.

Its designers claim in particular a simplicity of use that is not at the expense of performance. Using the library as is, without changing the default parameters, should lead to the generation of a model with good performance. The native support of categorical features is not unrelated to this ease of implementation.

### 9.4.1   Biases

**Selection of the feature and the decision criterion**

CatBoost uses its own method to select the most relevant feature/decision threshold pair when adding a node to a decision tree.

They call this method quantization, and it essentially consists of distributing the samples into buckets. This is similar to the LightGBM approach.

### Support for categorical features

By default, and if the number of features is not too large, CatBoost uses one hot encoding to integrate categorical features in its training, in the case of classification.

If it is a regression, in this case, the data sharing common categories are grouped into buckets, and these buckets are assigned a value. It is this value that will be used as a decision criterion.

### Parallelization and distribution

Like LightGBM, CatBoost supports fewer distribution frameworks than XGBoost: it is only compatible with Apache Spark.

### Hyper Parameters

CatBoost's hyperparameters overlap with those of XGBoost and LightGBM.

The names may change but the underlying principles remain the same.

### Choice and customization of the objective function

This is an important limitation of CatBoost: it does not allow you to manually define objective functions.

You have to be satisfied with the ones offered, which are however quite numerous.

### Interfacing

For the training part, CatBoost only supports Python and R, which is finally sufficient in most cases.

However, it is possible to reuse models from other languages, such as Rust, Java, or C/C++. The CatBoost team has taken care to keep the prediction time to a minimum so that it can be used in applications where latency must be minimized.

### Simplicity of use

The strength of CatBoost is its ease of use coupled with the guarantee of obtaining correct results.

It is also worth noting the explainability functionalities that are directly integrated into the library, and which accelerate the analysis of the performance of a model.

## Implementation language

CatBoost is also implemented in C/C++, for the same performance reasons as her two competitors.

## Support for missing values

CatBoost also supports missing values.

### 9.4.2   Example

As for the two previous implementations, the functioning of Cat-Boost is illustrated in the example of the socio-economic data of the UCI Adult dataset:

```python
# ch8_catboost_example.py
from catboost import CatBoostClassifier
from sklearn.model_selection import train_test_split
from sklearn.metrics import classification_report,
    confusion_matrix, accuracy_score
import numpy as np
import pandas as pd

train = pd.read_csv('data/adult.csv')
test = pd.read_csv('data/adult_test.csv')

features = ['age', 'workclass', 'fnlwgt', 'education',
    'education-num',
        'marital-status', 'occupation', 'relationship',
            'sex', 'capital-gain',
            'capital-loss', 'hour-per_week', 'native-
                country', 'income']
to_predict = 'income'

X = train[features]
y = train[to_predict]

X_train, X_validation, y_train, y_validation =
    train_test_split(X, y, train_size=0.7, random_state
    =42)
```

CatBoost supports categorical data, so there is no need to apply pre-processing. Providing the categorical column names is enough:

```python
categorical_features_indices = np.where(train.dtypes !=
    np.float)[0]
```

```python
model = CatBoostClassifier(cat_features=
    categorical_features_indices)
model.fit(X_train, y_train, eval_set=(X_validation,
    y_validation))

pred = model.predict(test[features])
print(classification_report(test[to_predict], pred))
# Name:  income, Length:  16281, dtype:  object
# precision recall f1-score support
#
# <=50K 1.00 1.00 1.00 12435
# >50K 1.00 1.00 1.00 3846
#
# accuracy 1.00 16281
# macro avg 1.00 1.00 1.00 16281
# weighted avg 1.00 1.00 1.00 16281
print(confusion_matrix(test[to_predict], pred))
# [[12435 0]
# [ 0 3846]]
print(accuracy_score(test[to_predict], pred))
# 1.0
```

The performance obtained with the default values is excellent since the model is not making errors.

CatBoost keeps its promise of the simplicity of use. Out of three libraries, it is the one that requires the least number of lines of code.

# Chapter 10

# Multi-model approach

## 10.1 Global model

This book concludes with the presentation of two original model-building methods. In the first one, the generated organic model is no longer made of a single model, but of a combination of several.

Until now, all the models presented and built in this book were global.

In the second approach, the trained model remains global but is optimized for particular perimeters and resolutions.

### 10.1.1 Principle

The principle of this type of model is simple: a single model handles the globality of the data.

It does not matter if the underlying data can be grouped according to a specific criterion, it is up to the model to identify these group specificities with the help of features.

Decision trees are good candidates for this type of model because the essence of their operation is precisely to partition the data into subsets and to apply different corrections for these subsets.

### 10.1.2 Motivations

The major interest of this approach is its simplicity. The data are aggregated in a single dataset, which will allow the training of a single model.

The prediction is then done using this simple model.

## 10.2   Local model

### 10.2.1   Principle

The principle of this modeling mode is based on the division of the training data into as many datasets as there are possible resolutions.

To give a simple example, in the case of real estate sales price predictions, the data can be split by city, and a model can be trained by city.

In the same spirit, the classification of parts into defective or not categories can be done part type by part type.

### 10.2.2   Motivations

The interest of such a local approach, as opposed to modeling with a single model, which is global, is to focus the model on particular data, sharing common characteristics and distinct from other groups.

This avoids noise from one type of behavior with data from another type of behavior. Indeed, in the global approach, the prediction is built by starting from a basic prediction, the base_score, and successively improving it by applying different estimators.

When different types of data constitute the same training base for a single model, then there is porosity between several potentially different logics. The quality of the prediction can then be affected.

Another benefit that the data scientist gets from a local approach with several models is a much better understanding of the problem studied.

Indeed, each model will allow us to shed light on the behavior of such or such set of data and to identify the features that govern the behavior of each.

### 10.2.3   Application cases

This type of modeling can be successfully applied in many cases, as soon as samples of data are identified that can be grouped according to common characteristics.

### 10.2.4   Identification of resolutions

The identification of common characteristics is sometimes immediate and can be established trivially by the data scientist.

It is thus natural to split datasets by type of customer, product, room, region, and city. It is also interesting to work by age class, price, surface, volume, ...

It is also possible to work with different time grids. A model by month, week, or semester is sometimes relevant.

When these groupings do not seem obvious, it is fruitful to look at the data using other machine-learning tools.

Clustering methods are an excellent way to group samples with a common character before modeling.

In the case of time series, for example, clustering applied on automatically extracted temporal features generally offers good results.

### 10.2.5   Limitations

Several limitations should be kept in mind when using this method.

The first one is the extra computation time generated by the pre-processing of as many datasets as there are possible resolutions. For example, if it has been decided to create a model per city, and the training data contains thousands of cities, thousands of training datasets will have to be generated.

This additional cost is also found in the model construction phase, since here again the number of models must be multiplied by the number of resolutions.

The same pitfall is also found during the prediction phase.

The second disadvantage lies in the loss of information that can result from this division. If it is too artificial, part of the common information can be lost, and not benefit each model. This results in a loss of performance in the end.

In the extreme case where the partitioning becomes too fine, the size of the datasets can be reduced to such an extent that training is no longer relevant, or even possible.

Finally, in general, working with a multi-model approach increases the complexity of the whole process, and requires a well-built tool to manage the whole process robustly and reliably.

## 10.3   Global Optimized Model

There is a third way, which can sometimes combine the advantages of the two previous approaches.

### 10.3.1   Principle

The essence of this method is to train only one model, but then to adapt it during the prediction for each resolution considered.

For this purpose, the training phase is instrumented to monitor the performance level resolution by resolution, depending on the addition of new trees.

The optimal number of trees for each resolution is then used for prediction.

## 10.3.2　Motivations

The interest of this approach lies of course in the combination of the advantages of the two previous methods: uniqueness and thus simplicity of the model with the added bonus of the finesse brought by a multi-model approach.

## 10.3.3　Operation

The idea for this approach is to log during the training phase, at each addition of a new estimator, the performances for each of the considered resolutions.

This is a costly operation in terms of computation time, but it allows a fine analysis of the behavior of the model according to the chosen resolutions.

From this point of view, it is necessary to be able to use a custom evaluation function in the training phase. XGBoost among others allows this.

It is also necessary to be able to indicate during the prediction how many trees can be combined. XGBoost also allows this.

The code listing below shows how to perform this instrumentation of the performances of a model, during its construction, as the trees are added, and this resolution by resolution:

```python
import pandas as pd
import matplotlib.pyplot as plt
from xgboost.sklearn import XGBRegressor
from sklearn.datasets import make_regression
from sklearn.metrics import mean_absolute_error
from sklearn.model_selection import train_test_split

n_features = 40
X1, y1 = make_regression(n_samples=1000,
                         n_features=n_features,
                         n_informative=10,
                         noise=1,
                         random_state=42)

X2, y2 = make_regression(n_samples=1000,
                         n_features=n_features,
                         n_informative=n_features,
                         noise=1,
                         random_state=42)
```

```python
X1 = pd.DataFrame(X1, columns=[str(i) for i in range(0,
    n_features)])
X2 = pd.DataFrame(X2, columns=[str(i) for i in range(0,
    n_features)])

y1 = pd.DataFrame(y1, columns=['y'])
y2 = pd.DataFrame(y2, columns=['y'])

X1['VendorID'] = 1
X2['VendorID'] = 2

X = pd.concat([X1, X2])
y = pd.concat([y1, y2])
```

A dataset is constructed artificially, with two datasets, one of which, the first, is governed by fewer features. The distinction between these two datasets is done through an additional column, VendorID. This dataset is classically split into training and test datasets.

```python
X_train, X_test, y_train, y_test = train_test_split(X,
    y, test_size=0.2, random_state=42)
X_test = X_test.reset_index(drop=True)
y_test = y_test.reset_index(drop=True)
eval_set = [(X_test, y_test)]

v1_index = list(X_test[X_test.VendorID == 1].index)
v2_index = list(X_test[X_test.VendorID == 2].index)
```

The custom evaluation function is then added, to enrich the training phase with an evaluation of the predictions according to the two chosen resolutions:

```python
def multi_resolution_metric(y_pred, dtrain):
    y_true = dtrain.get_label()
    metrics = []
    mae_vendorID1 = mean_absolute_error(y_true[v1_index
        ], y_pred[v1_index])
    mae_vendorID2 = mean_absolute_error(y_true[v2_index
        ], y_pred[v2_index])
    return [('mae_vendorID1', mae_vendorID1), ('
        mae_vendorID2', mae_vendorID2)]
```

The model, an XGBRegressor here, is then trained, passing it the custom evaluation function:

```python
model= XGBRegressor(n_estimators=1500,
                    max_depth=2)
model.fit(X_train, y_train,
        eval_metric=multi_resolution_metric,
        eval_set=eval_set)
```
Finally, the results are analyzed through a graph:

```python
results = model.evals_result()

epochs = len(results['validation_0']['mae_vendorID1'])
x_axis = range(0, epochs)

fig, ax = plt.subplots()
ax.plot(x_axis, results['validation_0']['mae_vendorID1'
    ], label='VendorID == 1')
ax.plot(x_axis, results['validation_0']['mae_vendorID2'
    ], label='VendorID == 2')
ax.legend()
plt.ylabel('mae')
plt.title('Multi-model MAE')
plt.savefig('multi_resolution_metric.png')
plt.show()
```

The resulting figure is as follows:

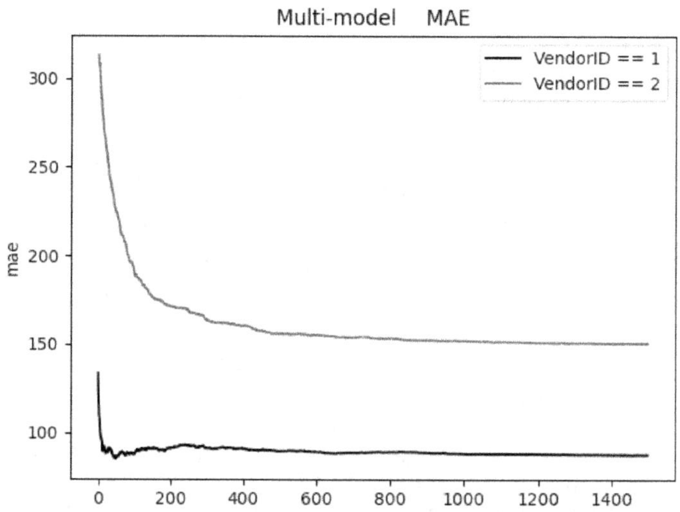


The latter clearly shows that for the first data set, the number of optimal estimators is around 50, while for the second set, not far from 800 trees are needed.

It remains then to make a prediction using first the maximum number of trees, then the optimal number, to estimate the benefit of the method:

```python
print(mean_absolute_error(y_test.iloc[v1_index], pred1)
    )
# -> 89.65769974171772
```

```python
print(mean_absolute_error(y_test.iloc[v2_index], pred2)
    )
#-> 156.0964928287915
print(mean_absolute_error(y_test.iloc[v1_index],
    pred1_opt))
# -> 85.22945890509138
```

Using the optimal number of trees for the given resolution does generate a performance gain, here of the order of 5%. This method is a good compromise of the two previous ones, often brings a gain in terms of precision, and offers in addition, through the analysis of the generated curves, a better understanding of the data.

# Chapter 11

# To go further

## 11.1  A broad overview

The subject of applying Gradient Boosting methods to the construction of decision trees has been covered from various angles and in-depth in this book.

Without being completely exhaustive on this vast subject, many points have been covered, from the theory to the application in various situations, including a scratch implementation, without forgetting the aspects of explicability, optimization of hyperparameters, and objective functions.

To deepen this knowledge, the author of this book can only recommend reading the original papers that usually accompany the source codes of the main libraries described here: XGBoost, CatBoost, and LightGBM.

The reading of these papers will allow us to further increase the mastery of this decision tree training technique, and to be able to bend it to more and more specific needs. In this way, it will be possible to refine the generated models more and more and to obtain ever better performances.

## 11.2  What to remember?

The objective of this book is to make the reader understand the theoretical framework in which Gradient Boosting methods are used.

In essence, what is important to remember is that :

- Objective functions drive the construction of trees. Playing with them is a powerful lever for building efficient models.

- Refining the hyper-parameters is a crucial step, which requires a detailed understanding of their role and the methodical construction of training and test datasets for cross-validation.

- Data enrichment is essential. Without data, it is impossible to build a model. The Gradient Boosting method only reveals its potential.

- Being able to explain a model is the key not only to its adoption by the recipient, but also an indispensable means to improve it.

- Time series require special treatment, because of their specific character.

- Since decision trees store constants in their leaves, they cannot extrapolate.

Finally, it is crucial to realize that this Gradient Boosting framework applies to decision trees but that it can be extended to other types of underlying models.

It is ultimately a very generic and powerful approach.

## 11.3   A field in constant evolution

The world of machine learning has been in constant evolution for a good decade now. Progress is daily from both theoretical and practical points of view.

New mathematical ideas emerge regularly to improve this or that point of the method, either to extend its field of application or to reduce the calculation time.

Innovations are also numerous on the technical and technological levels. These innovations make it possible, for example, to apply the method to larger volumes of data.

It is essential to keep up to date with these two types of developments and be reactive to take advantage of these advances.

To do this, the most effective way is to follow not only the sites dedicated to the main implementations but also some media or bloggers who are monitoring these topics.

## 11.4   Perspectives

Before closing this work, this last section will present some of the R&D avenues that should allow to further increase the possibilities of Gradient Boosting methods.

### 11.4.1 Coupling with neural networks

Gradient Boosting methods are often put in competition with neural methods such as Deep Learning.

The advantage goes to Gradient Boosting methods as soon as the data to be processed is structured.

The ease of configuration also benefits the latter.

On the other hand, the neural approach, and in particular the deep learning approach, offers an extremely attractive theoretical framework on the intellectual level.

Indeed, this same and unique framework allows us to build both the final part of a Machine Learning application, i.e. the regressor or the classifier, and the upstream part, i.e. the construction of features.

Coupling the two approaches is a promising track for improvement.

### 11.4.2 Differentiable programming

Objective functions are the core of the Gradient Boosting method. Through their gradient and hessian, the architecture and predictions of the generated trees are controlled.

The fact that differentiation techniques are already used suggests that this type of method could be integrated into the broader framework of differentiable programming.

In this framework, an entire program is seen as a function of many parameters, whose value would be fixed by permanent learning.

The determination of these values is done by deriving the whole program with respect to these parameters, and by using the gradient to converge to the optimal parameters.

The Gradient Boosting method fits naturally into such a framework.

### 11.4.3 Heterogeneous models

The essence of the approach proposed by Gradient Boosting is to combine weak predictors to build a strong predictor.

Until now, the libraries implementing this approach use the same type of model in an underlying way: decision tree, linear functions, ...

It would be quite possible to group within the same strong predictor a combination of different weak predictors.

Combining a decision tree with an SVM model and a linear function in an intelligent way with a Gradient Boosting approach should be possible.

Such an assembly of heterogeneous models would likely allow to reach even higher modeling levels.

# Index